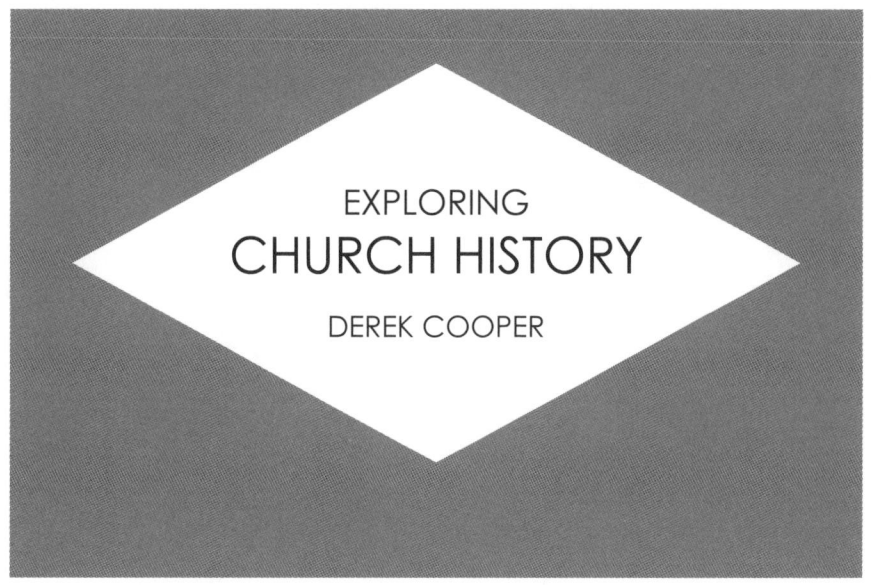

EXPLORING
CHURCH HISTORY
DEREK COOPER

This book is warmly dedicated to my parents, Robert and Gayle Cooper,
for all of their support and love. Although I have branched out,
I have not forgotten my roots.

EXPLORING CHURCH HISTORY

Copyright © 2014 Fortress Press. All rights reserved. Except for brief quotations in critical articles or reviews, no part of this book may be reproduced in any manner without prior written permission from the publisher. Visit http://www.augsburgfortress.org/copyrights/ or write to Permissions, Augsburg Fortress, Box 1209, Minneapolis, MN 55440.

Cover design: Laurie Ingram
Book design: PerfecType, Nashville, TN

Library of Congress Cataloging-in-Publication Data is available
Print ISBN: 978-1-4514-8890-6
eBook ISBN: 978-1-4514-8960-6

The paper used in this publication meets the minimum requirements of American National Standard for Information Sciences — Permanence of Paper for Printed Library Materials, ANSI Z329.48-1984.

Manufactured in the U.S.A.

Exploring Church History

Contents

List of Figures and Tables ix

Part 1: Why We Study Church History—Purpose 1

1. The Church Strives to Be *One* Family 5
   Welcome to *Your* Story: The Story of the Church 5
   The One Family of Christ Jesus: The Church 6
   Many Members of the One Family 8
   Practicing Hospitality toward Distant Relatives 10
   Conclusion: Family First 11

2. The Church Strives to Be a *Holy* People 15
   A Holy People? 15
   Holiness in the Bible 16
   A List of Grievances 18
   Repenting of the Unholiness of the Church 20
   Conclusion: Seeking to Become Holier 23

3. The Church Strives to Be a *Catholic* Body 27
   The Universality of the Church 29
   Three Ways to Become a More Catholic Church 31
   Conclusion: Embodying the Catholicity of the Church .. 35

4. The Church Strives to Be an *Apostolic* Church   39
   The Call toward Apostolicity   40
   The Difference between Progress and Alteration   42
   Insiders versus Outsiders?   44
   Conclusion: Wrestling with the Past   46

Part 2: What We Study in Church History—Content   **49**

5. A Tomb in Italy Illumines the History of Christianity
   in Western Europe   53
   The Story of a Tomb   54
   The Catholic Church   55
   The College of Bishops   58
   Devotion to Relics   60
   Conclusion: Still Adored after Nineteen Hundred Years   63

6. An Icon in Egypt Illumines the History of Christianity
   in the East   67
   The Story of an Icon   68
   A House Divided   69
   Icons in the Orthodox Faith   73
   The Monastic Movement   75
   Conclusion: Christ the Almighty Reigns   77

7. A Stele in China Illumines the History of Christianity in Asia   81
   The Story of a Stele   81
   The Church of the East   84
   The On-Again, Off-Again Church   86
   The Collision between Eastern and Western Worldviews   88
   Conclusion: Christianity in a Museum?   91

8. A Crucifix in the DRC Illumines the History of Christianity
   in Africa   95
   The Story of a Crucifix   95
   The Church in Africa   97
   Cultural Clashes between African and European Christians   103
   Conclusion: Lingering Questions   105

9. A Cloak in Mexico Illumines the History of Christianity in Latin
    America   109
    The Story of a Cloak   110
    The Social Context of Latin America   111
    Devotion to the Virgin Mary   114
    Bridge between European and Indigenous Cultures   117
    Conclusion: What a Difference a Cloak Can Make   118

10. A Warehouse in California Illumines the History of Christianity
    in North America   121
    The Story of a Warehouse   122
    American Pentecostal Churches   123
    Revivalism in America   127
    An Interracial Church   129
    Conclusion: From Warehouse to World   133

11. A Boot in Fiji Illumines the History of Christianity in Oceania 137
    The Story of a Boot   138
    Christianity in the Isles   140
    Foreign and Domestic Missionaries   142
    A Clash of Civilizations   144
    Conclusion: The Holy Clash Continues   147

Part 3: How We Study Church History—Method   151

12. A Medieval Forgery Illumines How to Write a Paper
    on Church History   155
    The Story of a Medieval Forgery   155
    Getting Started on a Research Paper   158
    Collecting Sources   159
    Formulating an Argument   160
    Overcoming Barriers   162
    Conclusion: Becoming a Budding Church Historian   163

Figures and Tables

Figures

Chapter 5—Saint Peter's Tomb in Saint Peter's Basilica
in the Vatican. The tomb is located directly below the main altar
of the church, Rome. Holger Weinandt, 2003.　　　　46

Chapter 6—The oldest known icon of Christ Pantocrator,
a sixth-century encaustic icon from Saint Catherine's Monastery,
Mount Sinai.　　　　60

Chapter 7—Reproduction of drawing of the text from Nestorian
Stele, Xi'an, China. The stele was originally engraved in 781 CE.　　　74

Chapter 8—Early seventeenth-century, copper-alloy cast crucifix
from the Kingdom of Kongo. Two figures atop Jesus and one
below him, all in prayer.　　　　88

Chapter 9—Image of Our Lady of Guadalupe in Mexico City's
Basilica of Our Lady of Guadalupe. Tomasz Pado, 2007.　　　102

Chapter 10—The Apostolic Faith Gospel Mission on Azusa Street in
1907. Apostolic Faith International Headquarters, Portland, Oregon.　114

Chapter 11—Thomas Baker exhibition at the Fiji Museum in Suva.　128

Chapter 12—Thirteenth-century fresco depiction of Constantine
"donating" his empire to Sylvester and the church.

Tables

Table 5.1—Ranks in the Catholic Church   54

Table 6.1—Branches of Orthodox Churches   65

Table 6.2—Commonalities among the Orthodox Churches   66

Table 7.1—Four Early Christian Church Traditions That Widened
over Time   79

Table 9.1—Historic "Caste System" in Latin America   106

Table 9.2—Four Dogmas of the Virgin Mary   108

Table 11.1—Division of Oceania into Major Regions   133

PART
1

Why We Study Church History—Purpose

Many church history books I have studied begin their stories with the assumption that their readers know why they are reading the book. This one does not. Although I consider the topic of church history to be interesting, useful, and important, others do not recognize the immediate and inherent value of this academic discipline. This is understandable, especially given that a portion of the public regards history as boring and the church as irrelevant.

So why should you study church history? In this part, I root my response to this daunting question in the history of the church—a rather brazen if not circular approach, to be sure. We study the history of Christianity, in part, so that we may embody the four characteristics of the church as suggested in the New Testament and codified at the Council of Constantinople in 381. The Nicene Creed, which the council reformulated at this council and circulated to the global church, has been in constant use in churches in all pockets of the globe since that time. In the creed, after the prior sections on God the Father, Jesus the Son, and the Holy Spirit, it delineates the "four marks" of the church: its oneness, holiness, catholicity, and apostolicity.

In each of the four chapters in this part, I offer a response to why you should study church history. Although I use the original language given in the creed, I also fully recognize that the church has not perfectly lived out its vocation to be one, holy, catholic, and apostolic. Nevertheless, I suggest that we study church history for four reasons: because the church is our family, because church history allows us to learn from our mistakes, because Christians from different time periods and time zones give us needed perspective, and because the study of the church's rootedness in Christ goads us on to faithfulness in the midst of changing cultures. I look forward to your company as we explore church history together!

Chapter 1

The Church Strives to Be *One* Family

S everal years ago, I attended a family reunion. Although held in Texas, where my father's side of the family has called home for six generations, relatives from other states and even foreign countries attended. During the two-day event, I spent most of my time with those I had known since childhood: my two brothers (of course), my first cousins, their parents, and my grandparents. However, I also socialized with second and third cousins, distant granduncles and grandaunts, and many other relatives reportedly once or twice removed from family members I scarcely knew existed.

At the reunion, I watched videos of great-grandparents who had died before I was born but who obviously played a pivotal role in my family's life. I heard heartwarming tales about my ancestors who immigrated to the United States in pursuit of their dreams. I listened to tragic stories about family members who had divorced, died prematurely, or otherwise experienced some calamity that left emotional scars on those closest to me. I held in my hands silver cutlery, porcelain dishes, and other articles my forebearers used. I glanced at photographs of people who looked eerily like me despite differences in hairstyle and wardrobe.

Welcome to *Your* Story: The Story of the Church

Studying church history is like attending a family reunion, but on a grander and even cosmic scale (Heb. 12:22-23). There are individuals from all nationalities, all walks of life, and all spheres of influence. There are those, like siblings and first cousins, whom we have known our entire lives, just as there are those, like third cousins and more distant relatives, with whom we are much less familiar. There are people we love to be around and others who are gossipers and rabble-rousers whom we hasten to avoid. There are stories too incredible to believe, too heartbreaking to ponder, and too sacrosanct to repeat.

The study of church history teems with stories of extraordinary courage and profound love, of shameful characters falling into disgrace and disrepute, of tragic events, innovative theories, world-defining movements and institutions, ancient rivalries, and family splits. It consists of ancient relics, faded pictures, half-standing buildings, theological apologies, autobiogra-

 What's your definition of "the church"? Depending on how you define it, it may include or exclude the holy departed who are now "in Christ" (1 Thess. 4:16) in the heavenly places. What role do the holy departed in Christ play in the church?

phies, Bibles, journals, letters, poetry and fiction, tomes, decrees, weapons, sacred vessels, frescoes, statues, sculptures, murals, graffiti, icons, cemeteries, castles and palaces, court records, wills, and remarkably enough, living relics like you and me.

Although it is sometimes dismissed as irrelevant or impersonal, church history is arguably the most relevant and personal subject in all of theology. It's a mega-story reverberating through the centuries and encompassing both you and me—and many others we will never know. It explains the most important and intimate features of our lives. It has given shape to our beliefs, worship practices, lifestyle choices, hopes and fears, and decisions concerning a whole cluster of issues related to our education, employment, friendships, marriage, and childrearing. In short, church history is a family affair. It's not simply a story that happened to someone in the past. It's *your* story, for it is intimately concerned with your other family—the church.

The One Family of Christ Jesus: The Church

In addition to our earthly families, whether biological or adoptive, the Bible speaks of a spiritual family united in Christ. This spiritual family is called "the church"—from the Greek *ekklesia*, more literally translated "the ones called out [of the world]." The apostle Paul, in one of his most poignant letters, proclaims to "all the members of God's family who are with me, to the *ekklesiais* of Galatia" that "in Christ Jesus you are all children of God through faith" (Gal. 1:2; 3:26). This dramatic declaration, particularly the second portion, serves as the crescendo of his argument in this brief letter—

 Did you know that, in Christ, you are related to some of the most interesting and inspiring individuals to ever walk the earth? How does their faithfulness affect how you live the Christian life?

and arguably of all of his letters in the New Testament. Despite economic, ethnic, linguistic, vocational, and gender distinctions among those living in Galatia, as elsewhere in the world, the Galatian Christians are "all one [family] in Christ Jesus" (3:28).

According to the Nicene Creed, the oneness of the family of Christ is the "first mark" of the church. The Christian church, the fourth-century document explains, is "one." The idea of the oneness of the church comes directly from the pages of the New Testament. In a celebrated passage that later Christians incorporated into the Apostles' and Nicene Creeds, the book of Ephesians underscores both the unity and the oneness of the family of God: "[Make] every effort to maintain the unity of the Spirit in the bond of peace. There is one body and one Spirit, just as you were called to the one hope of your calling, one Lord, one faith, one baptism, one God and Father of all, who is above all and through all and in all" (Eph. 4:3-6).

Over time, individuals and church communities from all parts of the world have affirmed belief in the oneness of Christ's family. In one of the earliest regional church disputes, a bishop in North Africa developed a theory of the church that still commands credence in many churches. The bishop's name was Cyprian of Carthage (c. 200–258). He lived in what is now Tunisia at the height of Christian persecution in the Roman Empire. In 251, he wrote a book titled *The Unity of the Church* to emphasize the oneness and indivisibility of the church. In the book, Bishop Cyprian famously asserted, "You cannot have God as Father without the Church as Mother."[1] Later in the book, he went on to write:

Although there is a small percentage of Christians today living in North African countries like Tunisia, Christianity was widely practiced throughout North Africa for centuries before the global expansion of Islam beginning in the seventh century CE.

God is one, and Christ is one, and his Church is one, and the faith is one, and the people are joined into a substantial unity of body by the cement of concord. Unity cannot be severed; nor can one body be separated by a division of its structure, nor torn into pieces, with its entrails wrenched asunder by laceration. Whatever has proceeded from the womb cannot live and breathe in its detached condition, but loses the substance of health.[2]

Although it is easy to get lost in the details, Bishop Cyprian was addressing an issue that directly affects Christians today, particularly in North America. This issue relates to the nature of the church—what is called ecclesiology. In effect, this North African bishop argued for the existence of only one family of Christ on earth—again, one church.

Many Members of the One Family

Most of us will not agree with all of Bishop Cyprian's conclusions, but the history of Christianity has safeguarded the concept of the oneness of the family of Christ despite the obvious fact that each century has witnessed church divisions, factions, splits, and reformations. At its most basic level, the oneness and the unity of the family of Christ refers, so to speak, not to the branches of the tree but to the root. Even though we come from the same rootedness in Jesus the Messiah, the spiritual family of which you and I are a part has sprouted many branches over its two thousand years of existence. Over time, some of these branches scarcely resemble one another. Finding commonalities between the Armenian Orthodox Church and the Mennonite Church, for instance, proves challenging. That's because a casual glance at their distinct expressions of theology and practice suggests more differences than similarities. However, as we look beyond the leaves, move aside some of the soil, and investigate the seeds that distinguish these two

Christian branches, we should begin to recognize their common rootedness in Christ.

Truth be told, the issue we are discussing is an ancient one that predates Christianity. We can address it in the form of a perennial philosophical question: What is the relationship between the one and the many—the universal and the particular? Once again, we may turn to the apostle Paul for a response to this question. In addition to the unity of the one church, Paul also wrote frequently about the diversity of that one family. "We who are many," he addressed to the conflict-ridden Christians in Corinth, "are one body" (1 Cor. 10:17). Later, in Paul's letter to the Christians in Rome, he developed this notion of diversity within unity: "For as in one body we have many members, and not all the members have the same function, so we, who are many, are one body in Christ, and individually we are members of one another" (Rom. 12:4-5).

Although Paul recognized the unity that believers share in Christ, he also oversaw and corresponded with churches from all around the Mediterranean. Due to ethnic, linguistic, and cultural differences existing among them across the Roman Empire, these churches no doubt differed on any number of issues. Paul, in fact, as a culturally intelligent global missionary, responded to issues that arose in his churches differently depending on the context—whether it was demanding that his disciple Timothy undergo circumcision out of consideration for the Jewish population or, contrariwise, prohibiting his disciple Titus from being circumcised in order to prove that Gentiles do not have to become Jews before becoming Christians (Gal. 2:1-3; 5:2-4; Acts 16:1-3).

Returning to the passage in Romans, Paul meant to underscore that Christians—particularly those living in fellowship together in the large and multicultural city of Rome—did not live or die unto themselves. Rather, they existed as one spiritual family whose different members served various functions and roles for the betterment of the whole community: "We have gifts that differ according to the grace given to us: prophecy, in proportion to faith; ministry, in ministering; the teacher, in teaching; the exhorter, in exhortation; the giver, in generosity; the leader, in diligence; the compassionate, in cheerfulness" (Rom. 12:6-8).

Although Paul was not speaking to the issue of church denominations, it is not unreasonable to conclude that the one family of Christ expresses itself faithfully through its distinct denominational members. According to this interpretation, the different theological "members" of the one body of Christ resemble different "gifts" that each church tradition or denomination displays. Put simplistically, each denominational member contributes a different gift to the one Christian body for its collective edification. It was under the oversight of the Coptic Orthodox Church in Egypt, for instance, that monasticism was born and spread across the global church—eventually leading to the preservation of countless Christian artifacts, documents, and Bibles. And it has been the Pentecostal churches in the past century that have transformed communities all over the known world, leading to the growth of Christianity in Africa, the Americas, and Asia.

Over time, individual churches and church traditions have gotten into the unfortunate habit of taking their one or two gifts away from the global Christian community in order to use them for themselves. This is understandable to an extent, but the result is that individual churches and traditions not only harbor suspicion toward other Christian traditions but also produce a form of theological greed in which we hoard gifts given for the whole church for ourselves. John Donne (1571–1631), an English author who became an Anglican priest, famously wrote in one of his poems, "No man is an island entire of itself; every man is a piece of the continent, a part of the main."[3] Told from one perspective, church history is the study of various ecclesial islands floating in a sea of theological division and distrust. Rather than building bridges between the islands and sharing our individual gifts with our distant relatives, we have often gone the way of ignoring the actual existence of these islands or of maligning the way they operate as well as the distant relatives who govern them.

Practicing Hospitality toward Distant Relatives

One of the benefits of studying church history is the opportunity it affords us to practice hospitality toward distant theological relatives. It is easy and natural for us to think only about ourselves and those closest to us, but it does not seem to exhibit the kind of love that the New Testament enjoins. As 1 Peter exhorts us, "Above all, maintain constant love for one another, for love covers a multitude of sins. Be hospitable to one another without complaining. Like good stewards of the manifold grace of God, serve one another with whatever gift each of you has received" (4:8-10).

If it is true that "love covers a multitude of sins," one might make the argument that we could yield our "correct doctrine" for the sake of love. Is there ever a time when it is better to intentionally sacrifice doctrine for the sake of love, specifically when it comes to non-essential doctrine?

The "constant love" about which this letter speaks to early Christians is linked closely with the demonstration of hospitality toward other Christians, likely believers who came from other churches.[4] The Swiss Reformed theologian Karl Barth (1886–1968) once wrote, "Strange as it may seem, it is still true, that those who fail to understand other churches than their own are not the people who care intensely about theology, but [are] theological dilettantes."[5] The study of churches from other Christian traditions disabuses us of the notion that we can have a family without grandparents and great-grandparents—and granduncles and third cousins. It is not without reason that the Orthodox tradition has historically seen little difference between Catholics and Protestants, given that the latter came from the former and necessarily imprinted its DNA onto the Protestant churches.[6] As much as we may attempt to live out our theology on our own, we cannot deny the work of our ancestors in the past or the existence of our second and third cousins in the present.

Conclusion: Family First

To bring this chapter to a conclusion, I have attempted to answer in part the lingering question as to why we study church history. In short, we do so because the study of church history is the study of our family. The study of church history enables us to identify and connect with our spiritual family in a way that we would never do otherwise. It allows us to understand where we come from, who we are, and what we want our legacy to be. Like all family histories, of course, church history is full of factions, strife, and splits. These unsightly divisions mar the church's witness to the world and sever the members of our own body.

However, the study of church history forces us to investigate what we have in common with distant brothers and sisters in Christ and to celebrate those differences in the context of a former unity. It encourages us to repent of family discord, seek peace with Christian cousins from different family trees, and reflect on Jesus' prayer for the church to be one just as the Father and Son are one (John 17). And it encourages us to agree with the words of a fourth-century bishop of Barcelona named Pacian: " 'Christian' is my name, but 'Catholic' is my surname. The former gives me an identity, but the latter distinguishes me. By the one I am approved; by the other I am marked."[7]

Before we are Baptists or Catholics, Lutherans or Methodists, we are "Christians." That is, we come from the same Christian family that is rooted in Christ the Messiah. It is only afterward that we are to be "marked" by different denominations. By focusing unduly on the latter, we become estranged from our cousins and grandparents in Christ and sever a part of our selves, but by emphasizing our prior identity as Christians, we can begin to achieve the unity for which Jesus, Paul, and the earliest Christians endeavored and prayed.

 ## Questions for Personal Exploration

1. How would you think and act differently toward others who identify as Christians if you thought of yourself and others primarily as Christians and only secondarily as Lutherans or Presbyterians or Pentecostals?
2. Go back and read through each of the longer quotes from primary literature in this chapter. What is the sense you get as you read through them?
3. How important is "unity" in church history in general and your own church body in particular?
4. How could you and your church practice theological hospitality in a concrete and practical way?

 ## Resources for Deeper Exploration

Buschart, W. David. *Exploring Protestant Traditions: An Invitation to Theological Hospitality.* Downers Grove, IL: InterVarsity, 2006.

McGrath, Alistair. *Christian Spirituality: An Introduction.* Oxford: Wiley-Blackwell, 1999.

Noll, Mark. *Protestantism: A Very Short Introduction.* Oxford: Oxford University Press, 2011.

O'Collins, Gerald. *Catholicism: A Very Short Introduction.* Oxford: Oxford University Press, 2008.

Ware, Kallistos. *The Orthodox Way.* 2nd ed. Crestwood, NY: St. Vladimir's Seminary Press, 1995.

Zizioulas, John. *Eucharist, Bishop, Church: The Unity of the Church in the Divine Eucharist and the Bishop during the First Three Centuries.* Brookline, MA: Holy Cross Orthodox Press, 2001.

👓 Notes

1. Cyprian, *The Unity of the Church* 6.

2. Ibid., 23.

3. John Donne, "No Man Is an Island," *Meditation* 17.

4. John Elliot, *1 Peter: A New Translation with Introduction and Commentary*, Anchor Yale Bible Commentaries 37, part 2 (New Haven, CT: Yale University Press, 2000), 753.

5. Karl Barth, *The Church and the Churches*, new ed. (Grand Rapids: Eerdmans, 2005), 57.

6. The Russian Orthodox layman Alexi Khomiakov (1804–1860) once wrote that Protestants "are no more than developers of the Roman teaching. The only difference is that they have adapted it to suit themselves." Khomiakov, "On the Western Confessions of Faith," in *Ultimate Questions: An Anthology of Modern Religious Thought*, ed. Aleksandr Shmeman (Crestwood, NY: St. Vladimir's Seminary Press, 1965), 50.

7. Pacian of Barcelona, *Letter to Sympronius* 1.4. Because other denominations had not developed at this early stage to the extent they exist today, Pacian also intends his statement to identify him as orthodox rather than heterodox.

Chapter 2

The Church Strives to Be a *Holy* People

Recently, I stood atop the Mount of Beatitudes in the northern part of Israel, the site where many Christians believe Jesus delivered the Sermon on the Mount.[1] I would have liked to have forged an eternal memory that day with the way the Sea of Galilee glistened in the sun in the distance below or how the birds lined themselves atop the beautiful Franciscan church adorning the hill. Instead, I am haunted by the pointed words of our guide immediately after our group solemnly read aloud the Sermon on the Mount. "You want to know why I'm not a Christian?" he asked candidly after we emerged from silent prayer in awe of the sacredness of the place and of the majestic words Jesus had uttered two thousand years before. "It's because I've never met a Christian who actually lives out what Jesus said."

A Holy People?

One of the many remarkable statements Jesus makes in the Sermon on the Mount appears at the end of the discourse. "Every good tree bears good fruit," Jesus firmly states, "but the bad tree bears bad fruit" (Matt. 7:17). Reconciling this passage with many events in the history of the church is not easy. No one dares deny that Christians—both as individuals and as communities—have committed heinous and appalling crimes against God, humanity, and nature over the course of our history. If we are a tree, we have produced many, many bad fruits. To be fair, the tree of Christianity

Saints of the church like Amy Carmichael and Mother Teresa are beautiful flowers that have blossomed in the rocky soil of the world. They inspire the church to pursue the greatness of our calling as Christians through word and deed. Their "good fruit" also balances the "bad fruit" of Christian past.

has also sprouted many sweet, delectable, and life-giving fruits. Early Christians were known, in fact, for rescuing discarded babies, and many missionaries, including Amy Carmichael and Mother Teresa, gave their lives to serve and love the poor and the disenfranchised. Yet, regrettably, the bad clusters of fruits have often overshadowed the good ones.

With so many justifiable criticisms against the church, one of the most challenging words to utter when reciting the Nicene Creed has to do with its claim that the Christian Church is "holy." Few today would use this word to describe either the church at present or the church of the past. And although there is good reason to still regard the church as holy, we must fully recognize our "unholy" history and take responsibility for our collective actions. In this chapter, we will offer a second response to the following question: Why do we study church history? Whereas the first chapter responded that we study church history because it is the study of our spiritual family, this chapter emphasizes how the study of church history allows us to learn from our mistakes.

Holiness in the Bible

Holiness is a theme that runs throughout the Bible and spills onto the pages of church history. As worshipers of a righteous God, the people of God are designed to reflect God's holiness to the world around us. As the second-century bishop of Antioch named Theophilus (d. 181) wrote: "To the world which is driven and tempest-tossed by sins, God has given assemblies—holy churches, in which survive the doctrines of the truth. They are like island harbors of good anchorage; and into these run those who desire to be saved, being lovers of the truth."[2]

The church is supposed to be a holy refuge for a shipwrecked world. The First Epistle of Peter states to the Christians living in Asia Minor, "As he who called you is holy, be holy yourselves in all your conduct; for it is written, 'You shall be holy, for I am holy'" (1:15-16). Repeating a command given to the Israelites from the book of Leviticus, this passage underscores the biblical belief that the people who worship the triune God are holy or set apart from the world. In the book of Leviticus, different degrees of holiness existed. Most "holy" were the Holy of Holies in the Tabernacle, its accompanying furnishings, and the high priest who alone could minister in it. Less "holy" were the other parts of the Tabernacle, its accompanying furnishings, and the priests who ministered in it. Despite different degrees, however, God was the source of holiness, hence God alone made something holy or sanctified. As Leviticus repeats several times, "I am the LORD; I [alone] sanctify you" (20:8).

In the New Testament, the concept of holiness underwent development. For instance, whereas in the Old Testament the typical Israelite—that is, one who was neither a priest nor a Levite, nor undergoing a Nazarite vow, nor ritually impure—was regarded as "clean" (*tahor* in Hebrew) rather than "holy" (*qadosh*), this distinction collapses in the New Testament. Paul and Timothy's letter to the Philippians, for example, was addressed "To all the saints [literally, "holy ones"] in Christ Jesus who are in Philippi" (1:1), irrespective of profession or rank. In this way, any person indwelt by the Holy Spirit—whether a mortician or a minister, a butcher or a bishop—was equally regarded as a saint or "holy one."

Despite this radical difference between New Testament and Old Testament beliefs about who is holy, we should nonetheless assume that there are also similarities. The first commonality relates to the fact that, in the New Testament, holiness still derives from God alone (see Rom. 8; 1 Cor. 6; and 1 Thess. 4). That is to say, only God's "spirit of holiness" (Rom. 1:4) sanctifies a person. A second similarity between the Old and New Testaments has to do with the degrees of holiness that Christians display. Although the Holy Spirit designates a person as "holy" in terms of his or her standing before God, it is still true that the "works of the flesh" (Gal. 5:19) are fully operative in the lives of believers. Hence Christians display degrees of holiness, as it were, inasmuch as they submit to the Holy Spirit or to the flesh. And even though the "spirit of holiness" attempts to cultivate the "fruit of the Spirit" in the lives of Christians (Gal. 5:22-23), many rotten fruits have ripened on the Christian tree—among them impurity, hatred, enmities, strife, dissensions, factions, and the like (5:19-20)—as a result of the "works of the flesh."

The internal battle all Christians face between "the works of the flesh" and the "fruit of the Spirit" gives context to our discussion in this chapter.

Put simplistically, one could interpret the virtues of the history of Christianity as events where individuals and communities surrendered to the work of the Spirit, while the vices indicate moments when the church yielded to the work of the flesh—or even worse, "to the evil one" (1 John 5:19). This line of interpretation explains, in part, why so many bad fruits have fallen from the Christian tree without having to resort to the fruitless argument that those who committed heinous crimes were not "true Christians"—whether accurate or not. To use the words of theologian Martin Luther (1483–1546), Christians are simultaneously saints and sinners: "This tension [between the works of the flesh and the fruit of the Spirit] lasts in us as long as we live; though in one person it is greater, in another less, according as spirit or flesh is stronger."[3]

Whether or not this interpretation satisfies every evil event in the history of Christianity, it does allow us, on the one hand, to affirm the church's holiness (which it receives on the basis of God's holiness alone) and, on the

> John Wesley wrote in a booklet titled "A Plain Account of Christian Perfection" that he believed certain Christians could live such Spirit-filled lives that they never sinned. His ideas were adopted and developed among the so-called Holiness churches in America such as the Church of the Nazarene and the Wesleyan Church.

other, to fully recognize how often we fall short of the holiness enjoined upon the church from the Holy Spirit. The study of church history celebrates the lives of many individuals and communities that surrendered to the Spirit while it is also mindful of the many individuals and communities that indulged the flesh.

A List of Grievances

Now that we have discussed what it means to call the church "holy" despite its shortcomings, it is now incumbent upon us to discuss some of the church's failings and learn from them. Lamentably, we are all too familiar with criticisms leveled against the church. I, for instance, have spoken to individuals and classes about the Crusades, the Inquisition, the Holocaust, and the church's abuses of children, women, ethnic minorities, and the poor. At times, the list of grievances against the church is so long that the study of church history causes us to wonder if we have done more collective harm than good—especially when we include sins of omission (not doing what we should) along with sins of commission (doing what we should not). Too often, it seems, Christians look no different from those we denounce. Fully recognizing that the church has also done many good things, I offer the following list of some of the abuses and crimes that have been perpetrated by the church:

- The condemning and maligning of fellow Christians in councils, synods, and other church meetings, some of which ended in violence and even death
- Witch hunts and other violence (whether physical, emotional, or verbal) against women
- Countless battles and wars
- Countless "crusades" against perceived heretical or heterodox Christians as well as practitioners of other faiths
- Institutions such as the Inquisition designed to threaten and torture those considered to have strayed beyond orthodox Christian belief and practice
- Forced conversions and physical violence (mutilation, torture, and death) against those who opposed conversion to Christianity
- Sexual abuse, pedophilia, and rape by leaders of the church
- Violence against various Christian traditions
- Dissensions, factions, and church splits
- Exploitation of and violence against nature
- Missionary violence against the evangelized
- Hatred of people who look, act, or think differently
- Neglect of and abuses of the poor and other minority groups
- Aligning with the side of power
- Becoming the voice of the state rather than the voice of Christ
- Not speaking against known injustices
- Accepting and participating in human trafficking and slavery

Repenting of the Unholiness of the Church

The preceding list of grievances against the church brings shame on the body of Christ and taints its witness to the world. But rather than distance ourselves from the wrongs that the church has committed, based on the notion that "some other tradition" or "some other age of the church" perpetrated them, it is more responsible to acknowledge our collective culpability and repent of it. (During Jesus' earthly life, for instance, he did not bypass being baptized or flee from his calling to die for humanity, even though he committed no sin. Instead, he willingly took on the sins he had not committed.) To return to our original question as to why we study church

 As we think about communal forgiveness, slowly read the Lord's Prayer (Matt. 6:9-13). Underline every use of the words "our," "us," and "we." How do these pronouns—rather than "my," "me," and "I"—affect our communal understanding of the church?

history, it is partly so we can learn from the mistakes the church has made, so that we do not continue them. Many of us are familiar with the adage by the Spanish-American essayist George Santayana (1863–1952), "Those who cannot remember the past are condemned to repeat it."[4] Church history is the only theological discipline that allows us to collectively remember our past so we are not doomed to repeat those events that violate love for God or love for others.

The leading founder of the Jesuit Order or Society of Jesus, Ignatius of Loyola (1491–1556), wrote a book called *Spiritual Exercises* in the 1520s that has been in common use ever since. In this book, Ignatius organized spiritual exercises for Christians to perform over the course of a month. One of the exercises he included, called an "examination of conscience," applies directly to our discussion about the unholiness of the church. Among the five points to consider in the examination of conscience, three stand out as particularly relevant for remembering and then repenting of sinful events in the history of Christianity: "*The Second* [Point for making a general examination of conscience] is to ask grace to know my sins and rid myself of them. . . . *The Fourth* is to ask pardon of God our Lord for my faults. *The Fifth* is to resolve, with his grace, to amend them."[5] Although we commonly understand the concept of the church's holiness to be a position we maintain due to the character and work of God, it is equally important to regard the church's holiness as a goal we desperately seek but often fail to realize. By examining our collective conscience through the study of church history, we may resolve to rid ourselves of the church's sin, solicit pardon for our faults, and resolve to amend our ways.

As we rid ourselves of collective sin, seek pardon, and amend our ways, it is important to recognize that different "branches" of the Christian tree (to return to a metaphor from the first chapter) will make this examination of conscience in various ways. Due to the widespread diversity of ecclesial and theological traditions today, it is not possible for the universal church to act and improve all at once or all together. Yet recent memory offers many examples of individual churches and denominations that have repented of past sins and amended their ways. Out of a very long list acknowledged sins, I will include examples coming from the two largest denominations in the United States: the Southern Baptist Convention and the Roman Catholic Church.

The first example comes from a document issued by the Southern Baptist Convention in 1995 on the occasion of the denomination's 150th anniversary. In its "Resolution on Racial Reconciliation," the denomination acknowledged its complicity in supporting the enslavement of African Americans and in harboring racist attitudes and implementing racist policies. As a few lines of the document attest:

> Be it . . . RESOLVED, That we lament and repudiate historic acts of evil such as slavery from which we continue to reap a bitter harvest, and we recognize that the racism which yet plagues our culture today is inextricably tied to the past; and

> Be it further RESOLVED, That we apologize to all African-Americans for condoning and/or perpetuating individual and systemic racism in our lifetime; and we genuinely repent of racism of which we have been guilty, whether consciously (Psalm 19:13) or unconsciously (Leviticus 4:27); and

> Be it further RESOLVED, That we ask forgiveness from our African-American brothers and sisters, acknowledging that our own healing is at stake; and

Be it further RESOLVED, That we hereby commit ourselves to eradicate racism in all its forms from Southern Baptist life and ministry.[6]

In its continued attempt to eradicate racism, the Southern Baptist Convention in 2012 elected Fred Luter as its first African-American president, who cites improving racial harmony as one of his intended goals.

The second example comes from the Roman Catholic Church. Upon the consecration of Pope Francis in 2013, his first official papal visit outside of Rome was to a small island in the Mediterranean called Lampedusa, where thousands of Muslim North Africans have fled for refuge, often using insufficient floating vessels that have led to many deaths. In response to a recent mass boat drowning of Muslim refugees, the pope visited the island and commended both the Muslim immigrants and Christians on the island who have shown hospitality to them. In the homily he preached during the visit, Pope Francis warmly greeted the Muslim refugees: "I give a thought, too, to the dear Muslim immigrants that are beginning the fast of Ramadan, with best wishes for abundant spiritual fruits. The Church is near to you in the search for a more dignified life for yourselves and for your families. I say to you *O' scia*! [a friendly greeting in the local dialect]."[7]

In the context of his predecessors' hostile and violent rhetoric advocating the killing of Muslims centuries before, Pope Francis intentionally communicated to the world during his first official visit outside of Rome that the Catholic Church was committed to "ask[ing] forgiveness for the indifference [of the church] toward so many brothers and sisters," implying that Muslims and practitioners of other religions are the church's brothers and sisters. The significance of Pope Francis's words come into view when they are contrasted with Pope Alexander III's (r. 1159–1181) papal bull *Cor nostrum* against Muslims eight centuries before:

To any fighting [Christian] men, well suited to the defense of that land [the Holy Land], who go to those holy places with the fervor of devotion, and fight there for two years against the Saracens [that is, the Muslims] for the defense of the Christian name, we, trusting in the love of Jesus Christ and in the authority of the blessed apostles Peter and Paul, grant absolution for all their sins which they have confessed with contrite and humble hearts.[8]

Conclusion: Seeking to Become Holier

To bring this chapter to a close, we have chiefly been concerned with rec-onciling the church's holy standing in heaven with its unholy actions on earth. That is to say, despite the inherent holiness of the church based on God's holiness, we have committed many sins and made many errors from which we must repent and learn. Although speaking about Catholicism in particular, the following quote from theologian Lawrence Cunningham equally applies to the history of the Christian Church:

> [The history of Christianity] shows that in the recognition of the imperfect nature of the Church in this life, despite its equal conviction that the Church, as the rule of faith has it, is one, holy, catholic and universal, there was an equal deter-mination to re-form the life of the Church, to cleanse it of its most conspicuous failings, and to call it back to its mandate to be the visible presence of Christ on this earth. It says this as a duty given by its apostolic teaching. One way to say it is that the Church is one, holy, catholic and apostolic, but it can always be more unified, more holy, more universal, and more faithful to the apostolic preaching.[9]

When the dark events of the church's history are compared with the light of God's holiness, no one dares deny that the church can, and should, become more holy and more reflective of God's character. The recognition and confession of the source of the church's holiness—the triune God—should direct the church to its knees in prayer in order to become holier than we currently are. "This determination," continues Cunningham, "to remedy [the church's] defects has been often summed up by a little Latin tag: *ecclesia semper reformanda*—the Church is always in need of reform."[10] In short, we study church history because the awareness of our shortcom-ings goads us to become more holy and more repentant and more gracious toward others. It goads us to become the type of people who practice what we preach and live out what we teach, so that our good fruit may be widely apparent to all. Admittedly, the church has a long way to go, but with God's grace, we aspire to a life of holiness that shines forth to all.

Questions for Personal Exploration

1. How would you respond to someone who said he or she would never become a Christian because Christians are hypocrites, hateful, or excessively violent?
2. Go back and read through each of the longer quotes from primary literature in this chapter. What is the sense you get as you read through them?
3. How important is "holiness" in church history in general and your own church body in particular?
4. How can the church become more holy? Give some concrete ways that the church can become holier than it currently is.

 Resources for Deeper Exploration

Francis (pope). *The Church of Mercy.* Chicago: Loyola Press, 2014.

Jenkins, Philip. *Laying Down the Sword: Why We Can't Ignore the Bible's Violent Verses.* New York: HarperOne, 2011.

Jenkins, Philip. *Pedophiles and Priests: Anatomy of a Contemporary Crisis.* Oxford: Oxford University Press, 1996.

Webster, John. *Holiness.* Grand Rapids: Eerdmans, 2003.

 Notes

1. In the New Testament, the sermon is contained in Matthew 5–7, while a similarly called Sermon on the Plain appears in Luke 6:17-49.

2. Theophilus of Antioch, "To Autolycus," in *We Believe in One Holy Catholic and Apostolic Church,* ed. Angelo di Berardino (Downers Grove, IL: InterVarsity, 2010), 69.

3. Martin Luther, "Preface to the New Testament," in *Luther's Works* (Philadelphia: Muhlenberg Press, 1960), 35:337.

4. George Santayana, *The Life of Reason* (New York: Charles Scribner's Sons, 1920), 284.

5. Ignatius, "Spiritual Exercises," in *Ignatius of Loyola: Spiritual Exercises and Selected Works* (Mahwah, NJ: Paulist, 1991), 134–35.

6. Southern Baptist Convention, "Resolution on Racial Reconciliation on the 150th Anniversary of the Southern Baptist Convention," Atlanta, 1995, http://www.sbc.net/resolutions/899.

7. Deacon Keith Fournier, "Lampedusa: Francis, the Pope of Solidarity, Challenges Us To Recognize the Immigrant as Our Neighbor," July 10, 2013, Catholic Online, http://www.catholic.org/news/international/europe/story.php?id=51628.

8. *Cor Nostrum*, in *The Crusades: A Reader*, ed. S. J. Allen and Emilie Amt, Readings in Medieval Civilizations and Cultures VIII (Toronto: University of Toronto Press, 2010), 187.

9. Lawrence Cunningham, *An Introduction to Catholicism* (Cambridge: Cambridge University Press, 2009), 195.

10. Ibid.

Chapter 3

The Church Strives to Be a *Catholic* Body

he year was 1867. The Civil War had recently ended in the United States, and the country was attempting to resurrect itself from the ashes of corpses and devastation. President Abraham Lincoln, whose tenure as commander in chief from 1861 to 1865 coincided with the years of the war, had just been assassinated, and the new president, a Southerner who would soon face impeachment, sought to "reconstruct" the infrastructure of the southern states and rehabilitate the economy in the midst of the South's continued poverty, confusion, and deep bitterness. It would be a long road toward recovery.

One of the peculiar features of the Civil War—amply illustrated in sermons, speeches, and books—was that both sides, North and South, assumed and boldly claimed that God was on *their* side. To learn more about the *religious* nature of the Civil War, see Mark Noll's *The Civil War as a Theological Crisis* and Harry Stout's *Upon the Altar of the Nation: A Moral History of the Civil War.*

The country, in spite of the division of North and South that had led it to war, was overwhelmingly Christian in orientation, and many Christian pastors from both sides of the Mason-Dixon Line had played key roles in the war as apologists, speakers, soldiers, and chaplains. One of the pastors from the South was a white man named Robert Lewis Dabney (1820–1898). He was a Presbyterian theologian, educated in the best schools of the day, professor at the University of Texas, and founder of a seminary in Austin. During the war, he served as a chaplain of the Confederate Army and chief of staff to General Stonewall Jackson (1824–1863). Even after the war, this Virginia clergyman could not understand why the long-standing and allegedly salutary institution of slavery had caused such a commotion. So in 1867, in a rational attempt to justify his theological and political views, he calmly yet systematically argued against the astonishing hostility of the North toward the South in a book called *A Defense of Virginia*:

> To the rational historian who, two hundred years from now, will study the history of the nineteenth century, it will appear one of the most curious and outlandish notes of human opinion that the Christianity and philanthropy of our day should have given so disproportionate an attention to the "evils" of African slavery. Such a dispassionate observer will perceive that, while many other gigantic evils were rampant in this age, there prevailed a sort of epidemic fashion of selecting this one upon which to exhaust the virtuous indignation and sympathies of the professed friends of human improvement.[1]

Although we have not yet reached two centuries since Dabney penned these words, it is arguable that most "rational historians" today would completely reject his comments regarding slavery, finding them

 The 13th Amendment to the U.S. Constitution, adopted in 1865, abolished slavery. The amendment came on the heels of Abraham Lincoln's Emancipation Proclamation of 1863, which called for the end of slavery in Southern states.

not only extremely arrogant and historically inaccurate but also morally repugnant. In short, Dabney, as a Christian minister of the gospel and vocal advocate of slavery, maintained that he squarely based his views on the sacred Scriptures, and he went so far as to question the moral integrity of those who opposed slavery yet also affirmed the truthfulness of the Bible.

Given Reverend Dabney's intelligence, education, and Christian upbringing, we may pause and ask ourselves why contemporary Christians completely disagree with him. Today, in fact, only 150 years after the Civil War and the abolition of slavery in the United States, Christians regard slavery as evil and opposed to the nature of the gospel. We celebrate that slavery is prohibited, and look upon the institution as a permanent stain on America's past that bleeds over into social inequalities to this day. Yet if the evil of slavery is so apparent to us today, why did such clarity elude many Christians in nineteenth-century America, including Robert Lewis Dabney?

Among other reasons, such as bigotry and selfishness, we may attribute this lack of clarity to an insufficient recognition of the catholicity of the Christian Church, that is, the church's universal scope in respect to place, race, and space. Because the posture of many churches and theological traditions tilts toward isolation rather than inclusion, this chapter will offer a third reason why we study church history—namely, because it reminds us that we are not alone and that we need different branches of the church and different points of view to help us read Scripture, understand the nature of the church, and discern the best way to live out our theologies. Like Dabney, we are prone toward bias and defensiveness, and we need Christians from all across the world in all eras of the past to help us become better Christians who embody the fruit of the Spirit.

The Universality of the Church

According to the Nicene Creed, the third mark of the Christian Church is that it is "catholic." This Greek term, though more commonly used to refer to the Roman Catholic Church, literally means "according to the whole."

 Thomas Aquinas is regarded by Catholics as one of the greatest theologians of the church. He is honored as a saint and as a "Doctor of the Church," whose teachings have played a significant part in the development of Catholicism.

In this way, to call the church "catholic" is none other than to assert that the Christian Church is universal in scope—encompassing all corners of the globe, all ethnicities and cultures, and all believers throughout history. The Dominican theologian Thomas Aquinas (1225–1274) described the catholicity or universality of the Christian Church as follows:

> The Church is Catholic, i.e. universal, first with respect to place, because it is everywhere in the world. . . . Romans 1:8: 'Your faith is proclaimed in all the world.' . . . Secondly, the Church is universal with respect to the state of [humankind], because no one is rejected, whether master or slave, male or female. Galatians 3:28: 'There is neither male nor female.' Thirdly, it is universal with respect to time. For some have said that the Church should last until a certain time, but this is false, because this Church began from the time of Abel and will last to the end of the world. Matthew 28:20: 'And lo, I am with you always, to the close of the age.' And after the close of the age it will remain in heaven.[2]

Rather than representing one corner of the global map, one view from a theological tradition, or one stage in history, the catholicity of the church underscores why, for instance, the church in New Zealand does not exist in isolation from the church in Uganda, why the Greek Orthodox Church and the Evangelical Lutheran Church in America have much to learn from one another, why the traditionally male-dominated church needs to listen to the experiences and insights of women, and why the church in the fourth century still speaks to the church in the twenty-first century.

The first person to describe the church as "catholic" was an early Christian writer named Ignatius (d. 111). He served as the bishop of Antioch, the city where Christians received their name (according to Acts 11:26),

 Bishop Ignatius' letter to the Christians in Smyrna was just one of seven that he wrote to churches surrounding the Mediterranean as he traveled from Antioch to Rome. In Rome, he was tortured and killed for his Christian faith.

and was reportedly mentored by the apostle John. Bishop Ignatius used the term *catholic* in a letter he wrote to the Christians in Smyrna in Asia Minor. In the midst of a larger discussion about the evils of church "divisions," he wrote, "Wherever the bishop appears, there let the congregation be; just as wherever Jesus Christ is, there is the catholic church."[3] In this usage, the word *catholic* meant "universal," but by the end of the century, it became a technical term describing the universal church in distinction to regional and perceived heretical or heterodox churches.

As we study the New Testament, the universality of the church is the telos (goal) toward which we strive as the body of Christ. Whereas many New Testament documents speak about the good news of Christ tearing down walls of separation between Jews and Gentiles, other passages teach about the church's unity—and that the reinforcement of differences in social standing undercuts the inclusivity of the gospel. The church's catholicity also draws its inspiration from the last book of the Bible: "After this I looked, and there was a great multitude that no one could count, from every nation, from all tribes and peoples and languages, standing before the throne and before the Lamb, robed in white, with palm branches in their hands" (Rev. 7:9). Despite obvious differences today among Christians of various races and social classes and languages, the end result for the people of God is the same: that we become a chorus of different singers praising the triune God in harmony with one another.

Three Ways to Become a More Catholic Church

When put in proper perspective, the vision for the church is to be geographically worldwide and racially inclusive. Admittedly, the church rarely reflects the grandeur described in such passages from the book of Revelation. Far too often, our bigotry, narrow-mindedness, insularity, penchant for schism, racism, and geographic location prevent the collective celebration of different cultures and ethnicities in churches. However, it still remains our calling to embody the catholicity of the church in its entire splendor—in all regions of the world (geography), in all Christian traditions (theology), and in all eras of its life (history). Or as James Cone, one of the most prominent theologians of Black Theology, says it, "The Church of Christ is not [meant to be] bounded by standards of race, class, or occupation."[4]

The first way we must attempt to live out our vocation as a catholic church is by expanding our understanding of place. Too often, Christians on one end of the continent assume, whether intentionally or not, that they are the only Christians living in the world. Sadly, we seem to show little concern for Christians on other continents or, indeed, even in other parts of the same city or neighborhood who differ from us. Returning to the opening quote, a deficiency of place contributed in part to Reverend Dabney's belief that only Christians who supported slavery interpreted their Bibles faithfully.

However, if only Dabney had understood the catholicity of the church in terms of its worldwide design and extent—of its grandeur surpassing that of his own tradition and time and race—he would have been forced to recognize that previous Christian leaders had affirmed Scripture while simultaneously preaching against the enslavement of other human beings. The following excerpt from a sermon preached by Dominican priest Antonio de Montesinos (d. 1545) in 1511 to Spanish Christians living on the island of Hispaniola (now the Dominican Republic and Haiti) illustrates how his interpretation of love led him to regard slavery as incompatible with Christ's command to love others:

> Tell me, by what right or justice do you hold these Indians in such cruel and horrible slavery? By what right do you wage such detestable wars on these people who lived mildly and peacefully in their own lands, where you have consumed infinite numbers of them with unheard-of murders and desolations? Why do you so greatly oppress and fatigue them, not giving them enough to eat or caring for them when they fall ill from excessive labors, so that they die or rather are slain by you, so that you may extract and acquire more gold every day? And what care do you take that they receive religious instruction and come to know their God and creator, or that they be baptized, hear mass, or observe holidays and Sundays? Are they not men? Do they not have rational souls? Are you not bound to love them as you love yourselves? How can you lie in such profound and lethargic slumber? Be sure that in your present state you can no more be saved than the [Muslims] who do not have and do not want the faith of Jesus Christ.[5]

The second way to embody the catholicity of the church is by listening in humility to theological traditions, ethnicities, and cultures outside of our own. Even though we do not always recognize each other as faithful believers, the universal church is one family whose many relatives share a common last name—that of "Christian." Yet, this is oftentimes the opposite way we identify ourselves. Before we identify as Christians, we claim a prior and stronger identity as Baptists or Methodists, Africans or Europeans, Arminians or Calvinists. However, by recognizing as brothers and sisters those who call on the name of the Lord and accept the major tenets of the faith—rather than regarding them as heretics or schismatics or foreigners—we may make corrections to our own biases and blind spots.

We may take as an example the African American Christians over whom Reverend Dabney claimed rightful possession. Living within a white-dominated Christian society in the South, Dabney did not at all consider the plight of the minority African American church. Ideally, Dabney should have questioned what right any person had to own another human being, Christian or not. Indeed, we want to shout out to Dabney a question that John Wesley raised on the other side of the Atlantic Ocean in 1774 to white Christians perpetuating the institution of slavery:

> Are you a human being? Then you should have a human heart. But have you indeed? What is your heart made of? Is there no such principle as compassion there? Do you never feel another's pain? Have you no sympathy, no sense of human woe, no pity?[6]

If this question was not compelling enough for Dabney, claiming ownership over a person one regards as a fellow sibling in Christ and a child of the Most High should have been. Rather than exploiting a person for my benefit, I would be forced to put his or her needs above my own (Romans 12). By acknowledging this, we might be forced to agree with a comment a man from South Africa made in 1920 about Europeans: "Many white ministers had not come out here [to South Africa] for the good of the native, but for their own good."[7] The American institution of slavery reinforced distinctions between black and white, free and slave, rich and poor, blessed and cursed—the complete opposite of Paul's words to the troubled church in Galatia: "no longer Jew or Greek . . . no longer slave or free . . . no longer male and female" (3:28).

Finally, the third way the church may become a more universal body is by drawing from its rich theological heritage in the past as well as from Christians with different experiences in the present. To begin with, there is a tendency in American churches to unshackle ourselves from the past, live self-sufficiently, and ignore that generations of faithful Christians have lived before us in all corners of the world, and that we stand on the work they achieved. Not only that, these Christians of the past have much to teach us. The historical writings, personal stories, and spiritual disciplines of the church are a veritable treasure trove of encouragement, hope, wisdom, and needed perspective. We neglect the devotional and spiritual riches of previous Christians to our own detriment.

To return one final time to Reverend Dabney's comments about slavery during the era of the Civil War, it appears that his prior commitment to the state of Virginia and its unconditional defense of slavery leaked over into his reading of the New Testament and into his treatment of fellow human beings. One wonders how Dabney's patriotism would have affected his reading of the Bible had he been born in the free state of Massachusetts. We may catch a glimpse of this unbridled union between religion and politics in America from a French Catholic visitor named Alex de Tocqueville (1805–1859), who toured the United States in the 1830s: "When I arrived in the United States, it was the country's religious aspect that first captured my attention. The longer I stayed, the more I became aware that this novel situation had important political consequences. In France, I knew, the spirit of religion and the spirit of liberty almost always pulled in opposite directions. In the United States I found them intimately intertwined: together they ruled the same territory."[8] Although in the United States Christianity went hand in hand with politics, this was not the case in other parts of the world. Historically, Christians have been minorities in many parts of Asia and Africa. And in the West, there was precedence of Christian traditions intentionally questioning the role of the state in the church, and of minority groups in America calling into question discriminatory practices of the state. A failure to acknowledge the separation of church and state in different eras of church history possibly contributed to Dabney's defense of slavery for the good of Virginian citizens rather than the defense of enslaved Christians for the good of the gospel.

In addition to the church drawing from its catholicity by listening to saints of the past, we must not forget how much we may learn from contemporary Christians. One of the contributions of the past century has come from theologians who have brought race and gender to the forefront of discussions about theology. By listening to Christians today coming from various perspectives—as women, as Latinos/Latinas, as immigrants, as African Americans—we may open our eyes to discriminatory practices unwittingly perpetuated by those in positions of power. For example, James Cone has decried "the bankruptcy of any theology in America that [does] not engage the religious meaning of the African American struggle for justice."[9] Because Western theologians, who have been in positions of power for centuries across the world, have tended to focus on abstract ideas rather than social realities, the church must incorporate the insights from minority groups into its theologies in order to fully attain the catholicity of the church.

Conclusion: Embodying the Catholicity of the Church

To conclude this chapter, a third reason we study church history is that this study forces us to recognize that the particular form of Christianity we practice represents only one aspect of the universal church. We are incomplete and imperfect. In fact, no church or theological tradition can possess all the spiritual gifts or be free from error. Rather, like a scattered puzzle set, we exist in tandem with other Christian churches and traditions and find our self-identity, strength, and splendor only when linked with them. By studying the catholicity of the Christian Church, we gain necessary perspective, since we are all partial, finite, and biased people in desperate need of hearing and learning from Christians of different time periods, perspectives, and theological traditions. We need other Christians to point out our blind spots, prejudices, short-sightedness, and sin.

Although we have used the writings of Robert Lewis Dabney as an example of an insufficient understanding of the church's universal nature, we must not draw attention to the speck in our brother's eye while overlooking the log in our own: we are all guilty of neglecting the positive role Christians of the past have played in faith, maligning other Christian traditions for reading the Bible or expressing their beliefs differently, and ignoring the plight of other Christians around the globe or even in our own neighborhoods.

The truth is that we have much to learn from Christians of the past—and present. In the end, we must protect ourselves from declaring triumphantly that we are the only and most faithful Christians of all time, but rather recognize the universality of the church and its interconnectedness. As Bishop Augustine of Hippo (354–430) said in one of his sermons, "I include as many faithful Christians as are here, by the grace of God, in this church, that is, in this city, as many as are in this region, as many as are in this province, as many as are across the sea, as many as are in the whole world."[10] It is the study of church history that leads us to learn from and celebrate with faithful Christians in different regions of the world from different ecclesial and theological traditions along different stages in the past.

 ## Questions for Personal Exploration

1. Why do you think so many Christians read the Bible differently and understand theology differently than we do?
2. Go back and read through each of the longer quotes from primary literature in this chapter. What is the sense you get as you read through them?
3. What do you think the benefit would be to yourself and your community if you were to read on a regular basis from Christians of a different time period and theological tradition? What would be some potential challenges to this?
4. How important is "catholicity" in church history in general and your own church body in particular?

 ## Resources for Deeper Exploration

Di Berardino, Angelo, ed. *We Believe in One Holy Catholic and Apostolic Church.* Ancient Christian Doctrine. Downers Grove, IL: InterVarsity, 2010.

Dulles, Avery. *The Catholicity of the Church.* Oxford: Clarendon, 1985.

Kärkkäinen, Veli-Matti. *An Introduction to Ecclesiology: Ecumenical, Historical, and Global Perspectives.* Downers Grove, IL: InterVarsity, 2002.

Meyendorff, John. *Catholicity and the Church.* Crestwood, NY: St. Vladimir's Seminary Press, 1997.

Porter, Lawrence. *A Guide to the Church: Its Origin and Nature, Its Mission and Ministries.* Staten Island, NY: St. Pauls/Alba House, 2007.

◉⊙ Notes

1. Robert Lewis Dabney, *A Defence of Virginia* (New York: E. J. Hale & Son, 1867), 1.

2. Thomas Aquinas, *Opusculum VII*, "In Symbolum Apostolorum, scil., Credo in Deum, Expositio," in *The Catholicity of the Church*, ed. Avery Dulles (Oxford: Clarendon, 1987), 181.

3. Ignatius, *Smyrneans* 8:1-2, in *The Apostolic Fathers*, 2nd ed., ed. Michael Holmes (Grand Rapids: Baker, 1989), 112–13.

4. James Cone, Black Theology and Black Power (Maryknoll, NY: Orbis, 1997), 65.

5. "Human Rights in 1511?" in *Religion in Latin America: A Documentary History*, ed. Lee Penyak and Walter Petry (Maryknoll, NY: Orbis, 2006), 23–24.

6. John Wesley, "Thoughts on Slavery," in John and Charles Wesley: Selections from Their Writings and Hymns: Annotated and Explained, ed. Paul Chilcote (Woodstock, VT: SkyLight Paths Publishing, 2011), 245.

7. "South Africa: 'United We Stand, Divided We Fall' (1920)," in *A History of Christianity in Asia, Africa, and Latin America, 1450–1990: A Documentary Sourcebook*, ed. Klaus Koschorke, Frieder Ludwig, and Mariano Delgado (Grand Rapids: Eerdmans, 2007), 234–35.

8. Alexis de Tocqueville, *Democracy in America: A New Translation by Arthur Goldhammer* (New York: Literary Classics of the United States, 2004), 340–41.

9. James Cone, *The Cross and the Lynching Tree* (Maryknoll, NY: Orbis, 2011), xvi.

10. Augustine, *Sermon* 213.7. Quoted in "We Believe in One Holy Catholic and Apostolic Church," volume 5, *Ancient Christian Doctrine* (Downers Grove, IL: InterVarsity Press, 2010), 4.

Chapter 4

The Church Strives to Be an *Apostolic* Church

I n 1704, a woman living in modern Angola prepared for death as she lay in her bed with a severe fever. Baptized in the Catholic Church as a child, she was a proud Kongolese noblewoman whose ancestors had adopted the Christian faith from Portuguese missionaries two centuries earlier. The woman's name was Dona Beatriz Kimpa Vita, and she was twenty years of age. Though tightly gripped by death's hands, she miraculously recovered upon sight of an angelic figure that approached her bed. It was Saint

---

St. Anthony was born and raised in Lisbon, but later died in Padua, Italy. He was later proclaimed "Doctor of the Church" by the Catholic Church, and is regularly petitioned by believers for the recovery of lost items.

Anthony of Padua, a celebrated Portuguese priest of the Franciscan order, who had died in 1231. According to Dona Beatriz, the five-hundred-year-old saint spoke to her as follows:

> I am Saint Anthony, firstborn son of the Faith and of Saint Francis [of Assisi]. I have been sent from God to your head to preach to the people. You are to move the restoration of the Kingdom of Kongo forward, and you must tell all who threaten you that dire punishments from God await them.

> First I had gone into the head of a woman who was in Nseto,
> but I had to leave as the people there did not receive me well.
> . . . [Finally,] I am trying once more, this time in Kimbangu,
> and I have chosen you to do this.[1]

After finishing his speech, Saint Anthony walked toward Dona Beatriz, entered her head, and merged with her body. Under possession of the figure, Dona Beatriz heralded Anthony as the most important saint in Christianity as well as a member of the Godhead. Moreover, God told her that Jesus, rather than being born in Bethlehem, was born in the regal city of São Salvador, Angola, and that both he and his mother, Mary, were Africans from the Kingdom of Kongo, not Jews from Judea. In fiery sermons, Dona Beatriz denounced physical representations like crosses and statues of the saints, and she pleaded with the Christian king to restore his kingdom. Even after Kongolese forces arrested and burned her for heresy and witchcraft in 1706, the movement she had founded lingered for many years.

The story of Dona Beatriz and the Kongolese-Catholic-based movement she founded probes the boundaries of the Christian religion. At what point does Christianity become heresy? In what way does the Christian church maintain its orthodox identity amid diversity and plurality? How does the church stand on the work of the apostles while also responding responsibly to situations that the apostles never encountered? All of these questions are queries into the apostolicity of the church, and they ultimately lead us to the last of our reasons for studying church history—namely, to direct ourselves toward orthodox Christian faithfulness despite constantly changing contexts and cultures.

The Call toward Apostolicity

The term *apostolicity* comes from a Greek word that means "sent." The apostles were the earliest "sent ones" testifying to the life, death, and resurrection of Christ. They were harbingers of God's coming kingdom, appointed and empowered by Christ himself to lead, heal, and preach as he had done. The book of Ephesians declares that the church was "built upon the foundation of the apostles and prophets, with Christ Jesus himself as the chief cornerstone" (Eph. 2:20). In the book of Acts, the apostles featured prominently in the story of the early church. Acts reports that the growing number of believers "devoted themselves to the apostles' teaching" (2:42), and throughout the book, all authority lay invested in these individuals in matters of theology and practice.

After the death of the earliest apostles, Christians took great care to preserve the ancient traditions passed on to them from the first believers. Oftentimes this deposit of truth was called "the rule of faith," which was an amalgam of beliefs and practices the universal church adhered to that guided the interpretation of Scripture, especially when the biblical canon was in the process of development. The concept is based on passages in the Bible that seek to preserve the truth of the good news entrusted to the earliest apostles and their disciples. Putting itself into the sandals of Timothy, the church has historically attempted to "guard the good treasure entrusted to [it], with the help of the Holy Spirit living in us" (2 Tim. 1:14).

In around the year 434, a monk named Vincent of Lérins, who lived on an island near Cannes, France, wrote a book called *Commonitory*. It was concerned with the theme of apostolicity and of protecting the treasure entrusted to the church. In the book, Vincent noted that the universal church took great care to "hold that which has been believed everywhere [*ubique*], always [*semper*], and by everyone [*ab omnibus*]."[2] In more detail, he wrote, "We will follow *universality* if we confess that one faith to be true which the whole church throughout the world confesses; *antiquity* if we in no way depart from those interpretations which it is plain that our holy predecessors and fathers proclaimed; *consent* if in antiquity itself we eagerly follow the definitions and beliefs of all, or certainly nearly all, priests and teachers alike."[3]

Although the church has never agreed on all things, there is ancient and universal consensus on essential matters of the faith as found in documents such as the Apostles' and Nicene Creeds. Many Christians might also include the Seven Ecumenical Councils, especially the first ones. Combined, these theological essentials converge around a shared belief in God the Father as Creator, God the Son as the human and divine Savior of the human race, and God the Holy Spirit as the giver of life, as well affirmation of the one church of God that strives to live out the gospel in anticipation of God's coming kingdom.

The Difference between Progress and Alteration

Although it is true that the church's beliefs and practices flow from the apostles' teaching and that the many Christian members are one inasmuch as they confess and live out these essential beliefs and practices, it does not follow that the church has nothing new to say to current situations or that it cannot progress. On the contrary, we must distinguish, so to speak, between the foundation and the building blocks. To use the language of Paul, Jesus Christ is the "foundation" of the different churches in the history of Christianity, while the building materials differ according to context, purpose, and even the environment in which the building is made (1 Cor. 3:11-13). What this means practically is that not every church need look alike other than in the foundation. The building materials of each

> It was these building materials from 1 Cor. 3:11-13 that Martin Luther was referring to when he infamously called the book of James "an epistle of straw." What he meant was that, in comparison with a book like Romans or Galatians—which were made out of gold or silver—James was a book made from weaker materials. For more, see Derek Cooper, *Thomas Manton: A Guided Tour of the Life and Thought of a Puritan Pastor*, ch. 4.

church are at the discretion of the human architects—whether made out of brick, cement, mud, straw, or stone. Applied to real-life circumstances, we could say that one church affirms the gift of speaking in tongues, one affirms the administration of rice cakes and water in the Eucharist, one affirms the use of icons in worship, and another affirms the leadership of women in all ecclesial leadership positions. Though building on the same foundation, these different materials serve the needs of the community for which they are constructed. And oftentimes they are not transferable from one culture to another.

While it has been an ongoing temptation in world Christian history to regard the distinctives of church bodies as unbiblical novelties or deviations from a fixed set of practices, Christianity is not a formula that can be lived out in mathematical precision but rather a living organism that grows and morphs in conformity to its surroundings. The question, in other words, is not whether Christianity can progress or not, but in what way it can progress without losing its core identity. To return to Vincent of Lérins in his book *Commonitory*:

> But someone will perhaps say: is there no progress of religion in the church of Christ? Certainly there is progress, even exceedingly great progress! For who is so envious of others and so hateful toward God as to try to prohibit it? Yet it must be an advance in the proper sense of the word and not an alteration in faith. For progress means that each thing is enlarged within itself, while alteration implies that one thing is transformed into something else.[4]

If we conceive of the apostles' teaching as a seed, it is only natural to recognize that the fruit of the tree will necessarily grow into something that looks quite different from the seed. When seeds grow into fruit trees, we call it a progression, but when seeds turn into insects, we call it an alteration. And this is how apostolicity distinguishes itself from the unity of the Christian church. The church is *one* in a static sense while it is *apostolic* in a dynamic sense; that is, it is apostolic when the church progresses according to its nature, but not when it alters. For instance, we know by instinct and by experience that an apple seed can and should progress into an apple tree (whether it bears edible apples or not) but cannot alter into a worm.

Because the good news about Jesus Christ and the teaching of the apostles is a seed intended to grow and expand into new regions, we should not be surprised when the tree of Christianity develops one way on rocky ground and another in fertile soil, or forms one way when struggling to survive in the desert and another when planted next to a steady stream. People, as soil, provide different cultures and temperaments in which seeds may grow—and die. Naturally, a tree must grow in accordance with its nature, but one's environment may vary dramatically from region to region. My travels into churches across Africa, Asia, Europe, Latin America, and North America confirm that the tree of Christianity in Chad, China, and Colombia, for instance, differ in as many ways as they resemble each other, despite their common seeds.

All of this is to underscore that there is a sense in which the identity of the church is latent and can be released only over time and in increments.

This puts the church in a precarious position. On the one hand, it must preserve the seed entrusted to it. On the other, the seed entrusted to the church will never remain the same but will—and must—grow into some-

 If this concept is true, what are the implications for confessional statements and catechisms of denominations, which are always written at a fixed point of time and usually binding thereafter?

thing larger and different from what it originally came. Because it takes decades, and even centuries, for seeds to grow into healthy and strong trees, Christians of later generations can scarcely conceive of when the church was just breaking out of the soil like a newborn bunny peeping out of a hole before taking its first steps on its own and out of harm's way.

Throughout the history of the church, countless movements and traditions have appeared that differed so much from one another that new language was created by one group to categorize another. Terms like *anathema, blasphemy, heresy, heterodox, orthodox, liberal, progressive,* and *schismatic* have historically served as weapons that condemn and denounce groups that appear to deviate from our own groups. Although the Christian church must distinguish itself from other religions that reject what God is doing in the world through Christ, part of this categorization derives from an inadequate understanding of culture as well as an imprecise way to differentiate among theological essentials, convictions, and preferences. Another part of it has to do with the sociology of group identity, which develops by forming insiders who exist in clear contrast to outsiders.

Insiders versus Outsiders?

When it comes to church history, the following question surfaces at regular intervals: How does the church distinguish between "insiders" and "outsiders"? The answer, which is not universally recognized among different Christian groups, is that a body of religious adherents is regarded as part of the Christian church inasmuch as it is "apostolic"—that is, insofar as it is built upon the foundation of the apostles' teaching (with Jesus Christ serving as the very cornerstone) in the knowledge that this teaching is always growing and progressing but never altering and changing. To return to the analogy used throughout this chapter, a church is apostolic when its seed is good and the tree progresses according to its nature.

These two characteristics of an apostolic church correspond, to some extent, with the Roman Catholic distinction between *Tradition* and *traditions*. As contemporary theologian Lawrence Cunningham explains:

> There is a distinction to be made between Tradition and traditions. Tradition with a capital 'T' stands for that unchangeable witness and proclamation of the Gospel given to the Apostles . . . , while traditions, with a small 't,' are those changeable customs, laws, and practices which the Church had adopted over the centuries in order to facilitate and further their mission. Thus, just to cite some examples, the Catholic Church teaches as part of its irreformable Tradition that bishops are successors of the Apostles who are ordained to guide, teach, and sanctify the Church, while the fact that bishops are to be unmarried (that is, celibate) is an ancient tradition [that is, a small 't'] which could be changed. There is nothing essential to [Catholicism] that would prevent bishops (including the pope) and their priests from being married.[5]

There is a dynamic relationship between the church of today and tomorrow and the church of yesterday and yesteryear. For example, the full inclusion of women into ordained ministry, though a more recent phenomenon in the church's past, represents Christianity's ministry in a changing world. In other words, it is not necessarily an alteration. If we applied the terms Cunningham uses, it would represent a *tradition* that has developed in many churches—though not (yet) in the Roman Catholic Church or in some other traditions—in contrast to a *Tradition* that cannot change, such as belief in the Trinity. Lamentably, Christians have done a lot of harm to each other by not adequately distinguishing between Tradition and traditions, or between the seed and the tree. Because change can quickly turn into alteration and is more difficult to monitor, many church traditions have preferred to preserve seedlings rather than cultivate mature trees.

Of course, different Christian denominations continue to debate whether this statement is true or false. As with other important issues, it does not appear that the worldwide church will be of one voice concerning this matter anytime soon, if ever.

Conclusion: Wrestling with the Past

To return to the story of Dona Beatriz Kimpa Vita, a Kongolese woman arrested and burned alive in 1706 for Christian heresy, we ask the question to which we are now better prepared to respond: Did the movement she founded represent a "progression" or an "alteration" of Christianity? Naturally, as we have learned from our history, not all Christians will respond in the same way. Some Christians would regard her teaching as within the bounds of Christianity yet potentially dangerous. They might reason that her championing of Saint Anthony of Padua as the greatest of Christian saints, though myopic when it comes to all the saints in the history of Christianity, was not necessarily opposed to the seed of the gospel as long as she taught other matters of faith and practice advocated by other Christians. Nor was her disdain for physical representations such as crosses and statues. Other Christians, without condoning the way she was treated and killed, would argue that the apostolicity of the movement she founded fell outside of the bounds of Christianity for various reasons. Her belief that Saint Anthony was a second God who merged with her body, for instance, clearly stands in opposition to almost 1,700 years of church doctrine. Such Christians would therefore regard her teaching as an alteration of the rule of faith rather than a progression, since it did not satisfy the test of universality, antiquity, and consent, nor of growth without change.

Whatever the case, our discussion of apostolicity points to one of the reasons we study church history: to wrestle thoughtfully with the tough questions of the Christian faith as it develops over time and in new environments. This process involves both science and art. In terms of science, we measure our orthodoxy against our interpretations of the teaching of the apostles as found in the Bible and in the early tradition; in terms of art, we seek to envision how the church will look different in relation to its engagement with constantly changing contexts. To be sure, art and science overlap at each stage of questioning, and the responses to these questions abound and diverge—sometimes violently so, as the history of Christianity demonstrates. Yet every church, in the past as in the future, must undergo this process of determining how it simultaneously affirms the essentials of the faith while adapting to and progressing in its unique context.

 ## Questions for Personal Exploration

1. What would you classify as Christian "essentials"? Give an example of a tradition that you believe is an "alteration" of the Christian faith, rather than a "progression." What accounts for the alteration?

2. Go back and read through each of the longer quotes from primary literature in this chapter. What is the sense you get as you read through them?

3. Do you think you could improve upon the "Vincentian canon," that is, Vincent of Lérins's measurement of Christian orthodoxy in terms of universality, antiquity, and consent? How so?

4. How important is "apostolicity" in church history in general and your own church body in particular?

 ## Resources for Deeper Exploration

Congar, Yves. *The Meaning of Tradition*. San Francisco: Ignatius, 2004.

Cowan, Steven, ed. *Who Runs the Church? Four Views on Church Government*. Grand Rapids: Zondervan, 2004.

Dulles, Avery. *The Magisterium: Teacher and Guardian of the Faith*. Washington, DC: Catholic University Press, 2010.

Guarino, Thomas. *Vincent of Lérins and the Development of Christian Doctrine*. Grand Rapids: Baker, 2013.

Johnson, Luke Timothy. *The Creed: What Christians Believe and Why It Matters*. New York: Image, 2003.

McGrath, Alistair. *"I Believe": Exploring the Apostles' Creed*. Downers Grove, IL: InterVarsity, 1998.

Sanneh, Lamin. *Whose Religion Is Christianity?* Grand Rapids: Eerdmans, 2003.

Tennent, Timothy. *Theology in the Context of World Christianity: How the Global Church Is Influencing the Way We Think about and Discuss Theology.* Grand Rapids: Zondervan, 2007.

Van Harn, Roger, ed. *Exploring and Proclaiming the Apostles' Creed.* Grand Rapids: Eerdmans, 2004.

 Notes

1. John Thornton, *The Kongolese Saint Anthony: Dona Beatriz Kimpa Vita and the Antonian Movement, 1684–1706* (Cambridge: Cambridge University Press, 1998), 10.

2. Vincent of Lérins, *Commonitory* 2.5. Here I am using the translation in Thomas Guarino, *Vincent of Lérins and the Development of Christian Doctrine* (Grand Rapids: Baker, 2013), 2.

3. Vincent, *Commonitory* 2.6 (emphasis added).

4. Vincent, *Commonitory* 23.1; Guarino, *Vincent of Lérins*, 15.

5. Lawrence Cunningham, *An Introduction to Catholicism* (Cambridge: Cambridge University Press, 2012), 12.

PART

2

What We Study in Church History—Content

n the chapters of part 2, we seek to dirty our hands, as it were, through the interpretation of discovered articles of the past connected to Christianity. These articles come in all shapes and sizes—a grave here, an icon there, a piece of clothing over there. Like you and me, they tell stories about Christians in the past, but unlike us, they cannot speak for themselves. They require discovery and interpretation—often eliciting contrary responses from scholars whose background, biases, and training take them down different paths of understanding and explanation. Just as the Bible draws out as many interpretations as interpreters, so, too, the discoveries in church history create rival schools of thought of the past. As we study the objects of the past, we must always keep before us the more fundamental question of purpose: why we study these articles. As in the first part, we study these objects in the conviction that church history is a family affair and intimately connected to our own spirituality, a corrective to past abuses and events, a check on our blind spots due to theological myopia, and a motivation to stay on the narrow and straight path of Christian faithfulness.

The aim of these chapters is illumination, not encapsulation. When you walk in a dark room and light a candle, the light illumines part of the room but not all of it. In the same way, I have selected different artifacts in major world regions to illumine Christianity in each region without attempting to summarize it in a way that captures all of its distinctives. I fully recognize that no artifact can encapsulate all of Christian history, so I do not attempt the impossible. In writing an introductory book on church history, my goal is to allow important artifacts to tell *a part* of the Christian story in the hopes that you might later explore the complete history in more detail. On our rapid journey through the global history of Christianity, our first stop will be one of the most controversial discoveries in the history of the church!

Saint Peter's Tomb in Saint Peter's Basilica in the Vatican.
The tomb is located directly below the main altar of the church, Rome.
PHOTO: HOLGER WEINANDT. CC-BY-SA 3.0 LICENSE (WIKIMEDIA COMMONS).

Chapter 5

A Tomb in Italy Illumines the History of Christianity in Western Europe

I n around 325 CE, the first Christian emperor of the Roman Empire examined plans for the construction of the most elaborate church in the ancient world. A dozen years had passed since Emperor Constantine (r. 306–337) had legalized Christianity in the Roman Empire, and several churches of varying conditions and styles were scattered across the Mediterranean. In the capital of the empire, these unimpressive churches paled in comparison to the grand temples and public basilicas that adorned the pagan-laden "Eternal City." Before long, Constantine landed on the location of the project: Vatican Hill, formerly a pagan cemetery, on the west bank of the Tiber River outside of the city.

> The Edict of Toleration, issued in 311, ended persecution of the Christian religion following the Diocletian persecution. Two years later, in 313, Constantine and Galerius regarded Christianity as a legal religion in the Roman Empire in the so-called Edict of Milan.

The emperor's decision to build a church over a pagan religious site was controversial and no doubt cost him political capital to disrupt the remains of countless Romans. To complicate matters, Vatican Hill had to be leveled. It is estimated that the operation required the relocation of more than a million cubic feet of soil as well as the construction of several large walls. Legend has it that Constantine moved twelve buckets of dirt in honor of the twelve apostles. By about 360, decades after Constantine's death, the church was complete. Although other magnificent churches in Rome and elsewhere were under construction after the legalization of Christianity in the early fourth century, this new basilica had something these other churches could not rival: Below the altar of the newly constructed church rested the bones of Saint Peter himself—the first pope, the successor to Christ's throne, and one of the greatest relics of the Catholic Church.

The Story of a Tomb

Sixteen hundred years later, in the early twentieth century, the map of the world had changed dramatically, and the Roman Catholic Church was competing with a rapidly changing society. The year was 1941. The world was entering a war of epic proportions—again. In Italy, at the height of power of the dictator Benito Mussolini, locally known as *il Duce* ("the leader"), Pius XII (r. 1939–1958), universally known as *il Papa* ("the pope"), issued an order from his tiny stretch of land atop the former Vatican Hill cemetery. Upon the workmen's discovery of a mausoleum in January 1941, Pius XII ordered a group of experts to secretly excavate the tombs below the altar of Saint Peter's Basilica, where tradition held that the bones of Peter himself lay.

During the dig, something unexpected happened. In the evening hours of 1942, after the experts had ended their excavations for the day, the project manager (Monsignor Ludwig Kaas) patrolled the excavations with his assistant as usual. During this patrol, however, he unexpectedly removed a set of bones from a marble coffin that had yet to be discovered by the experts. Along with his assistant, Monsignor Kaas relocated the bones with the intention of burying them once the excavation was complete. For ten long years, the bones lay in an unknown box without anyone discovering them. In the midst of those ten years, Monsignor Kaas died, and the group of experts found another set of bones they believed to be Peter's. The excitement generated by the excavators led Pope Pius XII, on Christmas Eve of 1950, to broadcast on radio that Peter's tomb had been discovered and that it was possible that Peter's very bones had been recovered. After the pope's death, however, a renowned anthropologist examined the bones and proved that they did not come from an elderly man from the first century. Meanwhile, the bones that Monsignor Kaas had secretly removed in 1942 still lay undisturbed and undiscovered in an inconspicuous, lead-lined wooden box.

This did not change until a new team leader discovered the box through a nonchalant conversation with the assistant in 1953. Through a series of events, the team leader gained approval from the new pope (the third one since the original excavations) to analyze the bones from Saint Peter's Basilica in the Vatican and also study the relics from Saint John's Lateran Basilica in nearby Rome, since an ancient tradition claimed that this basilica (and not Saint Peter's) contained the skull of Peter (but not the rest of his body). Although scientific evidence from the skull evaluated from Saint John's could not confirm with certainty that it matched the relics found in the tomb of Saint Peter's under the altar, researchers nonetheless concluded they were analyzing the very bones of the apostle Peter, the successor to Jesus Christ. Based on this research, Pope Paul VI (r. 1963–1978) in 1968, nineteen hundred years after Peter's martyrdom, made a shocking announcement: "New analyses—very patient and very detailed—have been made which led to results which, relying upon the opinion of competent and careful experts, we think positive: the relics of Saint Peter have been identified in a way which we consider as persuasive. It is our duty to announce to you and to the Church this happy news."[1] The "happy news" of the Vatican's discovery was unexpected, and many could scarcely believe that such a story was possible.

The Catholic Church

This story is filled with many twists and turns, and it stretches our imagination. Whether the researchers really discovered Peter's grave and remains or not, the story of the tomb in this dark cavern does serve as a useful way to throw light on the history of Christianity in Western Europe by highlighting Catholicism, the role of bishops (including the pope) in Catholic Christianity, and Catholic devotion to physical objects like relics. From its beginning, the Catholic Church was the primary tradition for most of Christianity's existence in Western Europe. In the first centuries after Christ, there was, of course, little difference between the so-called Catholic and Orthodox Churches; over time, however, as the church in the West institutionalized in accordance with its location, it gained a distinct identity.

The Catholic Church was born and grew into adolescence during the death throes of the mighty Roman Empire. Scholars now refer to the time period between the third and eighth centuries as the Late Antique period to emphasize its continuity with imperial Rome. Not surprisingly, the church adopted and adapted many existing ideas, structures, and terms from the skeletal empire. Without too much exaggeration, the bishop of Rome became a Christian version of the emperor, while other bishops were elevated to the Roman rank of *praetor* or magistrate. Dioceses (or bishoprics) were based on divisions of imperial administrations, and the dress of

---

Basilicas, and not Roman temples, made for a better model for Christian churches since basilicas could accommodate large numbers of people whereas Roman temples were small and designed only to house gods. How do you think Christianity would be different today if Roman Christians would have used temples, and not basilicas, as their architectural models?

---

bishops and priests developed from the secular dress of the Roman Empire. Money was funneled into dioceses, which created great wealth for the Catholic Church. Christian churches emulated the architecture of Roman basilicas, large public buildings used to conduct business or legal matters, by making the basilica their model for their worship spaces. Altars, based on ancient pagan shrines of the empire, became the centerpiece of all churches and the place on which the Eucharistic prayers were offered. Canon law reflected the legal code of the Romans, and early Christian preachers and writers took as their example the classical orators and authors of Greco-Roman antiquity.

Within a few decades after the conversion of Constantine to Christianity in the early fourth century, the church became the state religion of the empire. By the end of the fourth century, pagan sacrifice was banned, and emperors redirected a large part of the empire's revenues toward the ever-expanding budget of the church. Pagan shrines became Christian churches, and Christian saints and holy days were substituted for local deities and Roman holidays. The day of Christian worship, Sunday, was the day of the Sun ("sol" in Latin), a prominent god in the Roman pantheon. It's also possible that the *adventus* (Latin for "arrival"), a ceremony welcoming Roman emperors at the gate of a city after a military campaign, influenced the Christian season of Advent, when Christians welcomed the incarnation of their Lord into human flesh. Either way, Jesus' triumphal entry into Jeru-

 December 25, which is Christmas Day for Western Christians, was the date the ancients celebrated two different religious events. The first was Saturnalia, a winter solstice festival that included decoration of trees and gift giving. The other was the festival of *dies natalis solis invicti* "the birthday of the unconquered sun."

salem clearly echoed the Roman practice in the minds of early Christians. In fact, early Christian art resembled pagan art so closely that art historians cannot always distinguish Christian from pagan frescoes, murals, reliefs, and sculptures before the time of Constantine, such as the art found in the Roman catacombs. All of these issues take us back to our former discussion of apostolicity, and we must decide for ourselves whether early Western European Christianity represents a "progression" of the seed of the gospel or an "alteration." Clearly, the church in the West looked different in the Middle Ages than it did during the time of the first apostles.

Whatever the case, as the Catholic Church ventured into new areas in Western Europe—whether the British Isles, the Low Countries, or Scandinavia—it continued the practice of incorporating local beliefs and customs into Christianity. The bishop of Rome was regarded as the head of the Catholic Church, but regional bishops and abbots played important roles in the development of doctrine and devotional practices. Christian saints and the Virgin Mary held sway over the masses. In the Middle Ages, the creation of the university in Western Europe led to the prominence of professors and theologians. Despite the growth, prestige, and wealth of the Catholic Church, it faced its own controversies and struggles. From around the fourteenth to the sixteenth centuries, certain monks and theologians argued for reform. Although some stayed and made reforms within the Catholic Church, a segment separated and formed independent Protestant churches in the 1500s. These Protestant churches believed that they retained continuity with the seed of the gospel even when separated from the Catholic Church. Such churches flourished in regions farther removed from Rome (such as Germany, England, and Scandinavia), while those countries speaking Romance languages (such as France, Italy, Portugal, and Spain) retained Catholic cultures. Since this time, the Catholic Church has experienced unprecedented growth in Africa, Asia, and the Americas, and most Catholics today live well outside of Europe.

The College of Bishops

With such a large population of Catholics peppered throughout the world, we may ask why the headquarters of the Catholic Church still remains in Italy. The answer is not difficult to discover: when excavators below the ground floor of Saint Peter's Basilica analyzed mausoleum after mausoleum and bone after bone in the early twentieth century, they did not cease their excavation until discovering what they believed to be the relics associated with one man—Saint Peter. Unbridled respect for Peter emerged at an early date due to his close association with Jesus of Nazareth. From Jesus' calling of Peter along the Sea of Galilee in the late 20s CE, the impetuous fisherman accompanied him throughout his ministry. On one distinct occasion, immediately before he began his descent toward Jerusalem (that is, toward his crucifixion), Jesus allegedly designated Peter as his successor. As the notorious passage from the Gospel of Matthew states:

> Now when Jesus came into the district of Caesarea Philippi, he asked his disciples, "Who do people say that the Son of Man is?" And they said, "Some say John the Baptist, but others Elijah, and still others Jeremiah or one of the prophets." He said to them, "But who do you say that I am?" Simon Peter answered, "You are the Messiah, the Son of the living God." And Jesus answered him, "Blessed are you, Simon son of Jonah! For flesh and blood has not revealed this to you, but my Father in heaven. And I tell you, you are Peter, and on this rock I will build my church, and the gates of Hades will not prevail against it. I will give you the keys of the kingdom of heaven, and whatever you bind on earth will be bound in heaven, and whatever you loose on earth will be loosed in heaven." (16:13-19)

From around the third century onward, the Catholic Church used this passage to bolster its claim that Peter succeeded Jesus and that all of the popes who followed Peter were Jesus' rightful successors. Yet not everyone accepted this view. Writing at the turn of the fifth century in the East, Theodore, the bishop of Mopsuestia in modern Turkey from 392 to 428, reasoned, "This [authority] is not the property of Peter alone, but it came about on behalf of every human being."[2] Protestants would build upon this interpretation to lend legitimacy to their cause in the face of Catholic criticism that they had been severed from the one body of Christ and thus were heretics.

However we may decide to interpret this passage in Matthew, a related one from the Gospel of John generated a less controversial interpretation. When Jesus breathed on the disciples, imparted the Holy Spirit, and gave them authority to remit or retain anyone's sin (20:21-23), he did not designate one apostle but gave equally to all. From this concept developed the office of bishop. Ignatius, who was bishop of Antioch during late first and early second century and was reportedly discipled by John, the traditional author of the Gospel of John, classified the offices of the Catholic Church into three distinct categories: bishop, presbyter (or priest), and deacon. Referring back to our discussion on unity in the first chapter, Bishop Ignatius argued assertively that the unity of the church resided in the bishops: "So it is clear with respect to the bishop," he wrote to the church in Ephesus, "that we should view him as the Lord himself." And to the church in Magnesia (also in Turkey), he wrote that "the bishop leads in the place of God."[3]

Ignatius was bishop of one of the most ancient Christian cities, but there were other cities that commanded special prominence. The Greek term *pentarchy* ("leadership of five") refers to the earliest and most noteworthy bishoprics or dioceses (later, patriarchates) in Christianity: Rome, Constantinople, Alexandria, Antioch, and Jerusalem. The bishops of these cities were later called patriarchs due to their prestige and connections to Christian apostles. The five patriarchates maintained oversight of dozens of regional dioceses—and, in a theoretical sense, over every diocese of an authentic church. It was bishops (and no other officeholders) who presided over the Seven Ecumenical Councils from 325 to 787. Bishops were the true power brokers and gatekeepers of the Catholic and Orthodox Churches. It was believed that they were imbued with the authority to remit and retain sins, condemn heresies and heretics, confer the Holy Spirit upon individuals, determine right belief and practice, and authenticate a

Table 5.1 Ranks in the Catholic Church. Over the years, the Catholic Church has expanded its ranks, but those of bishop, priest, and deacon remain just as in the days of Bishop Ignatius.

Bishop of Rome (the pope, elected by the cardinals)
↓
Cardinal (honorary clerical position elected by the pope)
↓
Archbishop (bishop of a large diocese)
↓
Bishop (priest who oversees a diocese)
↓
Priest (pastor of a parish)
↓
Deacon (ordained office below priest at a parish)
↓
Laity (baptized and confirmed member of a parish)

---

church's existence. In the Catholic Church, bishops are orthodox inasmuch as they are in communion with the bishop of Rome, the pope.

Devotion to Relics

The last way the grave of Saint Peter illumines the history of Christianity in Western Europe is by establishing Catholicism's devotional link to physical remains. Ancient tradition claims that the apostle Peter served the Christian community in Rome as its first bishop. There he also became its most noteworthy martyr. It is commonly believed that Peter and several other Christians such as the apostle Paul were arrested in response to the unrelenting fire that devastated most of Rome in the summer of 64. The Greek apocryphal *Acts of Peter*, written around the year 200 in Asia Minor,

 The Acts of Peter also claim that Peter was persecuted and killed for teaching celibacy, especially to wives of prominent officeholders, and that he later appeared to the man who cared for his corpse after his death on the cross to rebuke him for spending too much money for his coffin.

narrates that Peter was crucified upside down out of deference to dying the same way Christ did.

Centuries later, the medieval *Liber Pontificales*, a "book of pontifical" rites performed by bishops, recorded that a second-century pope set up a shrine over the burial place of Peter, located in the Vatican Hill cemetery outside of the ancient city of Rome. For many years, ancient Christians inscribed their prayers into the plaster columns covering Peter's tomb. One such prayer, written in Latin in the early fourth century and accompanying a picture of Christ and Peter, prayed as follows: "Peter, pray to Christ Jesus for the holy Christian men buried near your body."[4] Around that time, when prayers to saints were becoming more and more common among Christians, Constantine ordered the construction of the most magnificent church building in Christendom: "Old" Saint Peter's Basilica. His construction of the church over the tomb of Saint Peter indicated that the spiritual power emanating from the saint's bones legitimated the church and gave the church its authority. And, according to Catholic spirituality, it did.

Strictly defined, a relic "is an object that was once connected with the body of a saint, martyr, or other holy person."[5] Theologically, the relic is like an aging bottle of wine that becomes stronger over time. "The yet-unused power of the dead saint still resides and ferments in them and can be tapped by the living."[6] From this side of the Enlightenment, modern readers have a hard time understanding the ancient and medieval fascination with physical objects such as relics. We modern readers sometimes forget, however, that the medieval world more closely resembles the world of the Bible than does the contemporary one. One historian, in fact, ponders whether denial of the power of relics is a denial of the afterlife itself—a key doctrine of Christianity: "To say that the miracle-working power of the relic . . . is macabre superstition is to deny the idea of the afterlife. To believe that the body part . . . channels the saint's beneficent and protective powers from the beyond to the here and now is merely to assert faith in the afterlife."[7]

Whether or not we agree with this author's perspective, a cursory reading of the biblical corpus gives way to several passages that take for granted belief in relics. For instance, we see relics in the story of Jacob's bones (Gen. 50:25-26) and in the story of Elijah's mantle (2 Kgs. 2:13-15). Better known, however, is the story connected with Elijah's successor and possessor of his mantle, Elisha. After a corpse was lowered into the grave of Elisha, the dead man "came to life and stood on his feet" just as "soon as the man touched the bones of Elisha" (2 Kgs. 13:21). Even in his death, Elisha was still working miracles through his relics.

In the New Testament, there are several stories associated with relics. The first is the puzzling episode recounting how tombs of the dead were opened and "many bodies of the saints who had fallen asleep were raised" (Matt. 27:52) as Jesus was dying. Commenting on this passage in the fourth century, Bishop Apollinaris asserted that Christ's death miraculously raised the bones of these dead saints. In another New Testament document, the Gospel of Mark tells the story of a woman who suffered from hemorrhages for a dozen years but was immediately healed after touching a piece of Jesus' cloak (5:25-34). Similarly, the miraculous powers of Peter were so prevalent in the book of Acts that people "carried out the sick into the streets, and laid them on cots and mats, in order that Peter's shadow might fall on some of them as he came by . . . and all of them were healed" (5:15-16). Finally, the apostle Paul was such a great wielder of power that even the handkerchief he used to wipe away his sweat (called a *sudarium* or "sweat cloth" in the Roman world) healed: "God did extraordinary miracles through Paul, so that when the handkerchiefs or aprons that had touched his skin were brought to the sick, their diseases left them, and the evil spirits came out of them" (Acts 19:11-12).

Building upon biblical passages such as these, relics became significant channels of power in the early church. After Polycarp, a second-century bishop from Asia Minor, was publicly martyred, his disciples lovingly preserved his bones, since, they claimed, such bones "were more precious than fine jewels and more refined than gold."[8] It was during the fourth century, however, that the cult of relics became fully fledged in the Roman Empire. Constantine's conversion to Christianity ushered in a new era. Not only were many new churches such as "Old" Saint Peter's Basilica constructed, but Constantine's pious mother, Helena, made a spiritual *iter* ("journey") to the Middle East and established the Holy Land as a major site of pilgrimage. All of a sudden, relics connected to the life of Jesus sprang up like flowers after spring rains.

Later that century, from one of the imperial Roman capitals in Milan, Bishop Ambrose (r. 374–397) claimed discovery of the relics of two martyrs and had them "translated" to the city, where they became the cornerstone of the new church. This new tradition exploded like wildfire. When relics of holy men and women were not dismembered and sold in the marketplace for private devotion, they were collected and carefully "translated" into important churches as channels of divine power for pilgrims and priests alike. Thousands of the faithful claimed divine healings from the relics, and the saints to whose bones the faithful prayed answered the requests of their devotees. The saints were like intimate friends, and their relics like treasured gold. Theologians of such renown as Augustine of Hippo, John of Damascus, and Thomas Aquinas heralded the veneration of relics and affirmed their ability to heal, while Catholic congregations and monasteries all over the world looked to the translation of saints' relics to give legitimacy and prestige to their places of worship.

Conclusion: Still Adored after Nineteen Hundred Years

In spite of the amazing relics that empower congregations and monasteries from India to Indiana, no collection of relics rivals those found in the Vatican. Yet after Pope Paul VI delivered the "happy news" in 1968 that Peter's bones had been persuasively identified, there were just as many skeptics as supporters. For countless millions, the news was met with incredulity and indifference. Questioning that these bones were indeed those of Peter, the mainline Protestant journal *The Christian Century* did not mince words: "But assuming that the bones are of the man Catholics consider the Prince of the Apostles and the first bishop of Rome, we, unlike Pope Paul, do not feel bound . . . to honor sacred relics. Indeed, we make no bones about the fact that we are perverse enough—Protestant enough—to believe that no bones, not even a saint's, are sacred."[9]

For many Protestant Christians, devotion to relics represents an "alteration" of the seed of the gospel. They believe such devotion promotes unholy practices that damage the apostolicity of the church. Despite the innumerable Doubting Thomases, however, Catholic author Thomas Craughwell may well be correct when he writes that critics' "objections have not persuaded a vast multitude of believers."[10] Regardless of whose bones remain sealed and visible twenty feet below the altar of Saint Peter's Basilica, they are still being venerated after nineteen hundred years in the conviction that somehow and someway, these old bones still serve as channels of new life from above.

Questions for Personal Exploration

1. Which model of church government do you prefer? How do you think you would respond if you found yourself in a church where the governmental authority was different?

2. Go back and read through each of the longer quotes from primary literature in this chapter. What is the sense you get as you read through them?

3. How would you narrate the history of Catholicism if you were teaching it to a class of Protestant Christians?

4. Can you think of any encounters you have had with Christian relics? How did you respond to the situation? Do you think you would respond the same way today? Why or why not?

5. If you are a Protestant Christian, what things what you emphasize if trying to live out the unity of the church with Catholic Christians? What things do the Catholic and Protestant churches have in common?

 **Resources for Deeper Exploration**

Bockmuehl, Markus. *Simon Peter in Scripture and Memory: The New Testament Apostle in the Early Church.* Grand Rapids: Baker, 2012.

Craughwell, Thomas. *St. Peter's Bones: How the Relics of the First Pope Were Lost and Found . . . and Then Lost and Found Again.* New York: Image, 2013.

Cunningham, Lawrence. *An Introduction to Catholicism.* Cambridge: Cambridge University Press, 2009.

Duffy, Eamon. *Saints and Sinners: A History of the Popes.* New Haven, CT: Yale University Press, 2006.

Freeman, Charles. *Holy Bones, Holy Dust: How Relics Shaped the History of Medieval Europe.* New Haven, CT: Yale University Press, 2011.

Hengel, Martin. *Saint Peter: The Underestimated Apostle.* Grand Rapids: Eerdmans, 2010.

Meyendorff, John. *The Primacy of Peter: Essays in Ecclesiology and the Early Church.* Crestwood, NY: St. Vladimir's Seminary Press, 1992.

Nickell, Joe. *Relics of the Christ.* Lexington: University of Kentucky Press, 2007.

◎⊙ Notes

1. Thomas Craughwell, *St. Peter's Bones: How the Relics of the First Pope Were Lost and Found . . . and Then Lost and Found Again* (New York: Image, 2013), 105.

2. Manlio Simonetti, ed., *Matthew 14–28*, Ancient Christian Commentary on Scripture, New Testament (Downers Grove, IL: InterVarsity, 2002), 45.

3. Ignatius of Antioch, "Letter to the Ephesians 6:1" and "Letter to the Magnesians 6:1," in *Ignatius of Antioch and Polycarp of Smyrna: A New Translation*, ed. Kenneth Howell (Zanesville, OH: CHResources, 2009), 79, 95.

4. John Evangelist Walsh, *The Bones of St. Peter: The First Full Account of the Search for the Apostle's Body* (London: Victor Gollancz, 1983), 85–86.

5. Joe Nickell, *Relics of the Christ* (Lexington: University of Kentucky Press, 2007), 13.

6. C. Stephen Jaeger, *Enchantment: On Charisma and the Sublime in the Arts of the West* (Philadelphia: University of Pennsylvania Press, 2012), 99.

7. Ibid.

8. "The Martyrdom of Polycarp 18.2," in Howell, *Ignatius of Antioch and Polycarp of Smyrna*, 171.

9. Quoted in Craughwell, *St. Peter's Bones*, 106.

10. Quoted in ibid., 110.

The oldest known icon of Christ Pantocrator, a sixth-century encaustic icon from Saint Catherine's Monastery, Mount Sinai. PHOTO: PUBLIC DOMAIN.

Chapter 6

An Icon in Egypt Illumines the History of Christianity in the East

I t was the sixth century. Justinian (r. 527–565) was ruling over an expanding Byzantine Empire from the enchanted city of Constantinople. Although he had inherited a kingdom plagued by religious division, he was making a name for himself. Besides influencing the liturgical tradition of the Orthodox Church, working tirelessly to unite the divided churches in his kingdom, and constructing a law code that would endure for centuries, Justinian is probably known best for the many building projects he commissioned. Chief among these buildings was the incomparable church of Hagia Sophia in Constantinople, dedicated in 537. On a more unassum-

> The Christian monks on Mt. Sinai were certainly aware that it was on this mountain where God prohibited the worship of images in Ex. 20, yet they devoutly venerated images. This shows us that early Christians interpreted prohibitions of image worship very differently *after* the incarnation of Jesus Christ.

ing scale, however, Justinian also ordered the construction of a monastery at the base of Mount Sinai, at the traditional site of the burning bush (Exod. 3:1-6). The monastery was completed in 565, the year of Justinian's death. It is possible that one of the last gifts the emperor gave was an icon of Christ to the newly built monastery. Whatever the case, this newborn monastery now possessed the oldest remaining icon in the world. In fact, the mountain on which God prohibited the making and worshiping of images was not only being used as a holy place to safeguard and make copies of images, it was being used a place to venerate them.

The Story of an Icon

The Christ Pantocrator family of icons, under which genre the icon referred to in this story falls, is one of the most iconic in Orthodoxy. The Greek term *Pantocrator* is literally translated as "All-ruler," but the word carries many layers of meaning. In the New Testament, the four living creatures in Revelation shout "Holy, holy, holy, the Lord God the Almighty [*Pantocrator*], who was and is and is to come" (4:8). The term is also used in the Nicene Creed: "We believe in one God, the Father Almighty [*Pantocrator*]." Although icons of God the Father are prohibited in the Orthodox tradition, since God does not have a body and hence cannot be imaged, the term *Pantocrator* was later used in the Byzantine Empire to refer to a specific style of Christ icons. In many ways, the Christ Pantocrator icons are the triumph of Byzantine Christianity and the celebration of Christ's dual (human and divine) natures in one body or person. This iconic tradition bears the wounds, so to speak, incurred during the spiritual battle that raged among different Christian bodies about the nature and persons of Christ as well as the validity of icon use.

The Christ Pantocrator icons are distinctive. With regional contrasts, they typically depict an adult Christ with a piercing gaze and stoic countenance; a halo or nimbus encircling the head signifies holiness. The left hand preserves the gospel, while the right hand gives a benediction by forming the first and last letters of Jesus Christ's name in Greek, ICXC—which would be rendered into English as JSChT, or **JesuS ChrisT**. As you come face to face with the Christ Pantocrator icon from Saint Catherine's Monastery at the base of Mount Sinai, you feel yourself pulled into the gaze of Christ. The lips are pursed together. Christ's hair is black and thick, and his beard is full yet not unkempt. Christ's nose is long and slender, and his face is asymmetrical. His left eye and cheek evoke the judgment of God, and the left eye brow is slightly raised. His right eye and cheek, meanwhile, emanate warmth and receptivity. Together, the two sides of his face hold in tension "the kindness and the severity of God" (Rom. 11:22), the dual natures of Christ the Almighty.

A House Divided

With many artifacts from which to choose, I have chosen the icon housed in Saint Catherine's Monastery in Egypt to illumine the history of Christianity in the Middle East and Eastern Europe since it surfaces the early divisions of the Orthodox faith, highlights the role of icons in Orthodox spirituality, and introduces monasticism in the development of Orthodoxy. Beginning with the first, the monastery that houses the Pantocrator icon is peculiar among historic monasteries in Egypt for its association with the Eastern Orthodox Church rather than the Oriental Orthodox Church, which is the overwhelming majority of Orthodox Christians in Egypt. While most Orthodox churches and monasteries in Egypt are part of the Coptic Church, the monastery at Saint Catherine's shows influence from both branches even though it is mostly autonomous.

As we have seen from the previous section, every major Christian family tradition has experienced not only disagreement among its members but also painful division and ecclesiastical divorce. In early Christianity, one of the most divisive stages of development occurred in the fourth and fifth centuries. The controversy revolved around how to express how Jesus was simultaneously God and a human being. Because there was no standard interpretation commanding agreement at this early stage, Christians offered different explanations of this mystery. Some Christians believed that Jesus was a man adopted by God the Father at his baptism. Others argued that Christ was a divine being whose body only appeared human. Still others suggested that Jesus' humanity and divinity merged together in full or, contrariwise, that they existed separately in his body like a husband and a wife living in the same household but never coming together.

Although this debate seems far removed from the struggles of contemporary Christians, it debilitated early Christianity because the entire economy of salvation hinged on how one decided the issue. You can decide for yourself: Does it matter if Jesus was not a human being, or if he was not

 Each of these councils occurred in modern Turkey and were conducted mostly in Greek. Violations of the theological conclusions drawn at these councils became a crime against the state, as there was no real division between the state and church at this time.

really God? For early Christians, they were prepared to base their earthly and eternal lives on their responses. It did not take too long, however, before some explanations prompted censure. An African priest in Alexandria named Arius (c. 250–336), for example, was convinced that Jesus was the first of creation but did not share the same "substance" with God the Father. His presiding bishop condemned him after hearing his views, as did the earliest global church councils, called Ecumenical Councils (dating from the years 325 to 787). If Arius's explanation was correct, his critics argued, then the church had been wrongly worshiping Jesus as God for three hundred years. And since this was not possible, Arius was wrong. Besides, there were just as many biblical passages supporting those opposed to Arius as passages in support of him.

On the other side of the spectrum was the interpretation offered by a bishop in Laodicea (or Latakia in coastal Syria) named Apollinaris (d. 390). As he looked into the mystery of the human and divine union, he imagined a Christ who was so full of divinity that he did not even possess a human mind. Apollinaris's desire to distance himself from Arius's views led him too far in the other direction. The problem with Apollinaris's interpretation, his opponents retorted, was that Christ could not have redeemed humanity unless he was fully human—that is, human in every way apart from sin (Heb. 4:15). As the Greek theologian Gregory of Nazianzus (329–390) wrote, "If anyone has put his trust in Christ as a Man without a human mind, he is really bereft of mind, and quite unworthy of salvation. For that which Christ has not assumed, He has not healed."[1]

As the debate about Christ's nature continued, a consensus was forming around the belief that Jesus was human *and* divine—not one or the other. There were, of course, spiritual casualties left remaining from the war toward consensus, but the global church seemed to agree on this front: Jesus has to be fully God and fully human. Unfortunately, the debate became even more heated and violent. From within the Orthodox family, a sibling rivalry among three different groups emerged. Using the names that are becoming more commonly known today, they represent the Eastern Orthodox branch, the Oriental Orthodox branch, and the Church of the East (or East Syrian branch), which are described in table 6.1. Even though these families disagree to this day on how to understand the relationship between Jesus' humanity and divinity, they were originally co-laborers of the faith who formed a unity based on the succession of bishops coming

Table 6.1 Branches of Orthodox Churches

Branch or Tradition	General Location	Individual Examples
Eastern Orthodox (also known as Byzantine or "Melkite")	Middle East and Eastern Europe	Greek Orthodox Church Bulgarian Orthodox Church Georgian Orthodox Church Russian Orthodox Church Serbian Orthodox Church
Oriental Orthodox (also known as Miaphysite or "Jacobite")	Middle East	Coptic Orthodox Church Ethiopian Orthodox Church Armenian Orthodox Church Syrian Orthodox Church
Church of the East (also known as East Syrian or "Nestorian")	Middle East	Assyrian Church of the East Ancient Church of the East Chaldean Church

from the apostles and on the common acceptance of the beliefs and practices coming from the Council of Nicaea (325) and the Council of Constantinople (381).

During the fourth and fifth centuries, this controversy reached climax. The next two Ecumenical Councils—the Council of Ephesus (431) and the Council of Chalcedon (451)—decided in clear favor of the Eastern Orthodox branch, which is by far the largest and best known of the Orthodox churches today. The first council condemned a bishop of Constantinople named Nestorius (r. 428–431), and although there was no direct connection between the two, the Church of the East was regarded as heretical because of its refusal to fully distance itself from Nestorius's views. The Church of the East also spoke and wrote in Syriac rather than Greek, which aided misunderstanding. At the next council, in 451, the Oriental Orthodox Church was condemned due to its views that Christ had one human and divine nature after his incarnation, rather than two distinct natures. Hence those Christians we classify under the nomenclature of the Oriental Orthodox Church were called Miaphysites ("one nature" in Greek).

Whatever the case, the division that occurred in the fifth century among the Orthodox Churches cannot be overstated, as it has led to an ongoing feud among these major bodies as well as centuries of maligning, misunderstanding, and resentment. As for geography, the Eastern Orthodox Church was the state church of the Byzantine Empire and the largest and most powerful Orthodox branch; the Church of the East existed outside of the domain of the Byzantine Empire and took as its goal the evangelization of greater Asia; and the Oriental Orthodox Church, before it was separated politically from the Byzantine Empire during the Muslim conquests of the coming centuries, became the most populous and vocal opponent to the state church. Once again, these divisions during the fifth century occurred in spite of the fact that these Orthodox bodies shared many commonalities, including accountability to the Nicene Creed and a common bond with one another within a larger Christian family (see table 6.2).

Table 6.2 Commonalities among the Orthodox Churches

- Unity and legitimacy through a body of ordained, male bishops with a line of succession going back to the apostles
- Similar styles of vestments, gestures, use of sacred space, and liturgical objects
- Daily office and liturgy
- The sacraments, including baptism of children followed by their chrismation and communion
- Prayers for the departed, especially after eight days, forty days, and a year
- Blessing and veneration of relics and icons, though the Armenians and the Assyrians venerate more often the cross
- Annual cycle of feasts
- Penitential and ascetical practices
- Kiss of peace
- Pilgrimage, especially to holy sites in Jerusalem
- Having a spiritual father
- No ordination of women to priesthood, though women deacons in the past were appointed

Source: Christine Chaillot, "The Ancient Oriental Churches," in *The Oxford History of Christian Worship*, ed. Geoffrey Wainwright and Karen Tucker (Oxford: Oxford University Press, 2006), 134.

Icons in the Orthodox Faith

Besides showing its Orthodox family tree, a second way the Christ Pantocrator icon illumines the history of Christianity in the Middle East and Eastern Europe is by underscoring the crucial role icons have played in Orthodox Christianity. In the past, as today, icons were typically painted on wood or embroidered on cloth. They offered a tangible piece of the Christian story well before the publishing of the Bible. For most of the church's history, in fact, Bibles were not widely available. Before the fifteenth century, all Bibles (indeed all books) were painstakingly copied by hand, usually by monks in monasteries. Purchasing a copy of the Bible would have

 How do you think your Christian faith would be practiced differently today if you did not have any access to a Bible? This was the reality for the "typical Christian" for the overwhelming majority of church history.

been cost-prohibitive for most Christians, unfeasible since most people could not read, and impractical for laypeople according to the culture of the day. Icons made theological assertions with as much clarity and vigor as any other medium. "An icon is a statement of faith, just like Holy Scripture or the theological formulas of the Liturgy."[2] Rather than with words, icons were "written" with light. The learned theologians cherished icons just as much as laypersons did, for they believed that Christianity was "the revelation not only of the Word of God, but also of the Image of God, in which His likeness is revealed [in icons]."[3]

Early Christians believed that Luke the Evangelist was the first one to "write" an icon. And even though we do not have any existing icons dating to this time period, "early Christian texts make it clear that icons were venerated by Christians from as early as 200 CE."[4] Their popularity increased in the fourth and fifth centuries. By the time the Christ Pantocrator icons were made in the sixth century at Saint Catherine's Monastery, the practice of making the portraits and pictures of the deceased as well as pagan gods was commonplace in Egyptian and Greco-Roman society.[5] This is not surprising. Just as early Christians used the language of the larger culture to worship God, so they made use of existing art practices. With the succession of

Christian rulers for generation after generation and the expansion of Christianity into new areas, pagan practices associated with portraits ebbed just as icon use among Christians increased and spread across the known world, having nourished Orthodox believers for both private and public devotion to this day.

In the eighth and ninth centuries, an imperially sponsored movement in opposition to the use of icons arose in the Byzantine Empire. Tension, including physical violence, broke out between the government-backed group that sought to destroy icons (iconoclasts) and the majority who preserved the use of them (iconodules). Referred to as the Iconoclastic Controversy, this bitter debate lasted for 150 years and even after the Seventh Ecumenical Council ruled in favor of icon use in 787. The most able defender of icons was a Syrian Arab Christian named John of Damascus (675–749), who lived outside of the Byzantine Empire and under Muslim rule.

From the Mar Saba monastery in Palestine, John argued that the prohibition against engraved images in the Old Testament applied only to Jews living before the incarnation of Jesus Christ, and that Jesus' assumption of flesh warranted the making of his image. He also adopted the existing belief that Orthodox believers do not worship the icon (for that is idolatry) but rather venerate (or honor) the one whose image is depicted in the icon. As John famously declared in his first apology against iconoclasts:

> In former times God, who is without form or body, could never be depicted. But now when God is seen in the flesh conversing with men, I make an image of the God whom I see. I do not worship matter; I worship the Creator of matter who became matter for my sake, who willed to take His abode in matter; who worked out my salvation through matter. Never will I cease honoring the matter which wrought my salvation! I honor it, but not as God.[6]

While Protestants historically looked upon veneration of icons as an "alteration" of the seed of the gospel, the Catholic and Orthodox traditions have regarded it as a "progression." Not only that, such traditions believe that use of icons protects the faithful from a heresy claiming that Jesus was a divine being whose body only appeared human. There is also something to be said for the fact that the Catholic and Orthodox traditions came into existence hundreds of years before the Bible was codified and widely available. This naturally played a role in their veneration of sacred objects beyond the Bible, since they believed that salvation, and the Christian life in general, was an inherently material or corporeal thing.

The Monastic Movement

One last way that the icon in Saint Catherine's Monastery in Egypt illumines Christianity in the Middle East and in Eastern Europe is through its connection to monasticism and a living worshipping community. It was in the Middle East that the monastic movement was born in the late third century. One of the pioneers of the movement was the Coptic Egyptian Saint Anthony (251–356). After he had entered the desert alone as a hermit to rigorously pursue the Christian life, he was later joined by many other spiritual athletes who wanted to learn from him as they sought intimacy with God in the desert. It was not long before the monks joined together to form monastic communities. Another Egyptian monk, Saint Pachomius (292–348), enclosed the individual huts of monks into one walled community and offered weekly instruction. The new community shared "a common refectory, kitchen, church, and garden where the monks grew their own food. They wore a monastic habit with a tunic, mantel [sic], and hood."[7] From this simple act, a new tradition was born—one that Protestant historian Mark Noll characterizes as, "after Christ's commission to his disciples, the most important—and in many ways the most beneficial—institutional event in the history of Christianity."[8]

The monastic movement soon spread all across the known Christian world. John Cassian (360–435) established a monastic community in France after living as a monk in the Middle East. Saint Simeon Stylites (390–459) lived atop a sixty-foot pillar in Syria for almost forty years. People from all regions and walks of life, including many who suffered from various diseases, came to listen to him preach, offer advice, pray, perform spiritual exercises, and heal from his perch. Later, Saint Simeon the New Theologian (949–1022) served as an abbot of a monastery in Constantinople. He developed a theology that emphasizes light (such as the light emanating from Jesus when he appeared to the disciples at the Transfiguration). In one of his many writings remaining today, Saint Simeon said:

Do not say: It is impossible to receive the Holy Spirit;
Do not say: It is impossible to be saved without Him.
Do not say that one can possess the Spirit without being aware
of it.
Do not say: But God does not appear to men.
Do not say: But men do not see the divine light—
Or at least it is impossible in this current generation.
This is a thing, my friends, which is never impossible, at any
time.
On the contrary it is entirely possible for those who long for it.[9]

Since the time of Saint Simeon, thousands of Orthodox monks have practiced rigorous forms of spirituality in monasteries around the world. One of the most famous clusters of monasteries in the Orthodox tradition houses about two dozen monastic communities in the northeast peninsula of Greece, which is called Mount Athos ("Holy Mountain"). Monks have called this stretch of land home for more than 1,500 years. Monastic communities like the ones in Mount Athos were (and are) the crucible in which the spiritual identities of countless renowned monks, priests, bishops, saints, and theologians have been shaped. In all Orthodox countries—whether in Bulgaria or Greece, Russia or Serbia, Egypt or Syria—monasteries play an important role in society and in the church.

In the Orthodox tradition, theology is the fruit of prayer and contemplation. Unlike the West, where theology has been severed from the spiritual roots of its liturgical community, the Orthodox faith keeps theology, spirituality, and worship indivisible. Orthodoxy keeps them inseparable

 Unlike the Orthodox Church, it is not uncommon for some prominent Western theologians to be unaffiliated with any Christian tradition, or indeed, to profess the Christian faith.

based on the ancient concept of *lex orandi, lex credendi* ("the law of prayer determines the law of belief"). The Orthodox tradition affirms what the Egyptian monk Evagrius Ponticus (345–399) concluded in his treatise on prayer: "If you are a theologian you truly pray. If you truly pray you are a theologian."[10] Monasteries, seminaries, and churches form a link, and there is no concept of theological reflection outside of the sacramental system and outside of the life of an active church body under the authority of a bishop who stands in the succession of the apostles of Christ.

Conclusion: Christ the Almighty Reigns

In my office, a Christ Pantocrator icon greets me as I come to work each day. It's a Russian Orthodox icon that depicts Christ holding a verse in the Russian language displayed from the Gospels. Although it portrays Christ in a slightly different way than the sixth-century Pantocrator icon in Egypt, it clearly resembles the original. For many Protestants, icons, crucifixes, and other ancient forms of Christian art threaten the truth of Christianity. The Bible—and the Bible alone—is often regarded as the only material object that a Christian needs in order to commune with God. Although Catholic and Orthodox traditions disagree with such a perspective, it is important to keep in mind that not only was the Bible unavailable to most Christians up until the past few hundred years, but much of the population would not have been able to read it, since the average person was illiterate. For the faithful majority, icons and other forms of Christian art were the primary conveyers of the narrative of Scripture.

Since the emergence of the Orthodox family of churches in the first century, this ancient tradition has spread around the globe. As for the Eastern Orthodox Church, it was centered in Turkey for a thousand years before it became dominant in Russia and other Eastern European countries. Although the Orthodox churches and monasteries across the world exhibit regional differences, they share a common identity. They also share a common story of tragedy, as many Orthodox nations have experienced their fair share of theological divisions from the inside and political threats from the outside. Despite such challenges, the Pantocrator icon, whether lovingly venerated or blithely unnoticed, proclaims with the full weight of the Orthodox Church that Christ "the Almighty" rules the world undeterred and unshaken.

 Questions for Personal Exploration

1. If you were explaining the history of the Orthodox Church to a Protestant audience, what things would you emphasize? Why?
2. Go back and read through each of the longer quotes from primary literature in this chapter. What is the sense you get as you read through them?

3. What should the relationship between the Eastern Orthodox and Protestants churches be, given that it was the former that codified the essential matters of belief for Protestant Christians today (in terms of convening and deciding the outcomes of the first Ecumenical Councils and the earliest creeds)?
4. Have you ever attended a church that venerated icons? How did that make you feel? How did this chapter help explain the importance of icons in the Orthodox community?
5. Referring back to the comment historian Mark Noll made near the end of this chapter, why do you think a Protestant historian stated that monasticism (which is not really practiced in Protestantism) was one of the most important events in the history of Christianity? Do you agree or disagree?

 ## Resources for Deeper Exploration

Bailey, Betty Jane, and J. Martin Bailey. *Who Are the Christians in the Middle East?* Grand Rapids: Eerdmans, 2010.

Bremer, Thomas. *Cross and Kremlin: A Brief History of the Orthodox Church in Russia.* Grand Rapids: Eerdmans, 2013.

Evseyeva, L. *A History of Icon Painting.* Moscow: Grand Holdings, 2005.

Louth, Andrew. *Introducing Eastern Orthodox Theology.* Downers Grove, IL: InterVarsity, 2013.

Martin, Linette. *Sacred Doorways: A Beginner's Guide to Icons.* Brewster, MA: Paraclete, 2002.

Ware, Timothy. *The Orthodox Church.* New ed. London: Penguin, 1997.

 ## Notes

1. Gregory of Nazianzus, "To Cledonius against Apollinaris (Epistle 101)," in *Christology of the Later Fathers,* ed. Edward Rochie Hardy (Louisville: Westminster John Knox, 1965), 218.

2. Andrew Tregubov, *The Light of Christ: Iconography of Gregory Kroug; Text and Photographs* (Crestwood, NY: St. Vladimir's Seminary Press, 1990), 12.

3. Leonid Ouspensky and Vladimir Lossky, *The Meaning of Icons* (Crestwood, NY: St. Vladimir's Seminary Press, 1982), 27.

4. Beth Williamson, *Christian Art: A Very Short Introduction* (Oxford: Oxford University Press, 2004), 10.

5. Nikodim Pavlovich Kondakov, *Icons* (New York: Parkstone Press International, 2008), 17.

6. John of Damascus, *On the Divine Images: Three Apologies against Those Who Attack the Divine Images* (Crestwood, NY: St. Vladimir's Seminary Press, 1980), 23.

7. Charles Frazee, *Christian Churches of the Eastern Mediterranean* (Placentia, CA: CreateSpace, 2011), 115.

8. Mark Noll, *Turning Points: Decisive Moments in the History of Christianity*, 2nd ed. (Grand Rapids: Baker, 2000), 84.

9. Quoted in John McGuckin, "The Eastern Christian Tradition (4th to 18th Centuries)," in *The Story of Christian Spirituality: Two Thousand Years, from East to West* (Minneapolis: Fortress Press, 2001), 147.

10. Evagrius Ponticus, *The Praktikos and Chapters on Prayer* (Kalamazoo, MI: Cistercian Publications, 1972), 65.

Reproduction of drawing of the text from Nestorian Stele, Xi'an, China.
The stele was originally engraved in 781 CE. PHOTO: PUBLIC DOMAIN.

Chapter 7

A Stele in China Illumines the History of Christianity in Asia

I n or around 1625, men digging a grave in the central Chinese country-side discovered a two-ton slab of limestone buried deep in the ground. Carved in the front with nineteen hundred Chinese characters as well as almost 150 personal names and words written in Syriac—a Semitic tongue akin to the language Jesus spoke—this stele measured nine feet high by three feet wide. The beautiful Chinese calligraphy inscribed on the stele was to be read from top to bottom and from right to left. At the trunk of the slab rested a giant tortoise, and at the top stood opposing dragons holding a pearl, adorned with clouds and a cross rising from a lotus flower. Though resembling thousands of others from China's past, this stele contained a story that those living could scarcely believe: it proved the establishment of Christianity in China around six hundred years before previously thought.

The Story of a Stele

Recognizing its ancient past, the diggers sent the stele about fifty miles to the modern city of Xi'an, which is located amid the ruins of Chang'an, the capital of several former Chinese dynasties. There the so-called Nestorian Stele permanently resides. As for steles, these were stone or wooden slabs used by governments in the ancient world to promulgate laws, designate temples and tombs, commemorate important events, delineate borders, and preserve writings such as the Chinese classic the *I Ching*. In China, where the Nestorian Stele was erected, tens of thousands of steles date from after the Tang Dynasty (618–907 CE).

One of these steles, publicly unveiled in the capital city of Chang'an on February 4, 781, narrates the arrival of a monk named Alopen (or Aluoben) in the year 635 from Persia who heralded a strange yet intriguing religion from the West. Alopen had traveled about three thousand miles with two dozen monks wearing white robes before entering the cosmopolitan city of Chang'an—the largest city in the world, with roughly a million inhabitants. At the top and in the middle of the stele, nine large Chinese characters organized in rows of three declare, "The Record of the Transmission of the Religion of Light of the West in China."[1] The Chinese characters used for Christianity, *jing jao*, combine the character for "light" or "luminous" with the character for "religion"—the same one used to refer to Buddhism and Daoism. The stele recounts the story of Jesus the Messiah, the first 150 years of Christianity in Tang China, and Emperor Taizong's (r. 626–649) official endorsement of this religion:

> The Way [Christianity] does not have a common name and the sacred does not have a common form. Proclaim the teachings everywhere for the salvation of the people. Aluoben, the man of great virtue from the Da Qin [Western] Empire, came from a far land and arrived at the capital [of Chang'an] to present teachings and images of his religion. His message is mysterious and wonderful beyond our understanding. The teachings tell us about the origin of things and how they were created and nourished. The message is lucid and clear; the teachings will benefit all; and they should be practiced throughout the land.[2]

In accord with this edict, many Christian writings were translated into Chinese. In 1900, for instance, a Daoist priest discovered a forgotten library in a cave in the ancient city of Dunhuang in the western region of China. Straddling the Silk Road, Dunhuang was once a booming town where merchants and missionaries traveled freely across the vast expanse of the Asian continent. Early in the eleventh century, someone sealed a cave in the town that contained several Christian writings (as well as many others) dating from the seventh to the eleventh centuries. Though stricken with time, these Christian scrolls display a vibrant and highly nuanced iteration of the Christian faith.[3] In one of the scrolls, a male figure—perhaps Christ or a saint of the Church of the East—resembles a Buddhist god yet is clearly a Christian because several crosses appear on his headgear, clothing, and staff. Several hundred miles west of Dunhuang in Qocho in northwestern China, an archaeologist in 1905 discovered three Christian murals dating from around the seventh century that corroborate the extent of Christianity in China.[4]

For reasons that are not totally clear, the "mysterious and wonderful" religion of Christianity failed to survive the Tang Dynasty, let alone the next several Chinese dynasties. By the time the Chinese dedicated the Nestorian Stele in 781, the seeds of the Tang Dynasty's demise had already been

---

Although Buddhism has existed in China at least since the middle of the second century CE and has incorporated itself comfortably into Chinese society, Buddhism originated in Greater India and is a foreign religion to China. Its beliefs and customs are quite different from native Chinese philosophies and religious such as Confucianism and Daoism.

---

planted. Empress Wu (r. 690–705), a usurper of her weak son's throne, made Buddhism the de facto religion and funded Buddhist communities and temples generously to the exclusion of the indigenous religions of Confucianism and Daoism. Upon her removal in 705, the next emperor restored the Tang Dynasty to its Confucian ideals and mounted an increasing attack against foreign religions such as Buddhism, Zoroastrianism, and Christianity.

In 845, an edict called for the confiscation or destruction of foreign religious places and the removal of priests and monks: "People belonging to [the foreign religions] are to be compelled to return to the world," it stated, "and belong again to their own districts and become taxpayers."[5] Possibly due to the persecution experienced at this time, Christians buried the Nestorian Stele adjacent to a seventh-century, seven-story Christian monastery (called the Da Qin Monastery), which has since become a Tower of Pisa–looking Buddhist pagoda. Although the edict of 845 was later reversed, the writing was on the wall for both Tang China and the Church of the East. After the fourteen-year-old emperor Ai (r. 904–907) witnessed all nine of his brothers killed by a commander named Zhu Wen (r. 907–912), he abdicated. So ended the Tang Dynasty—a dynasty that historian Samuel Moffett characterizes as "for the most part the friend of Christians."[6] Within a century of its collapse, a Christian speaking to a Muslim in Baghdad remarked, "There is not a single Christian left in China."[7] Although that statement was not exactly accurate, the Christian community in China was clearly vanishing. For the time being, the fate of the church in China paralleled that of the Nestorian Stele—dead in the grave until its resurrection several centuries later to the surprise and delight of Christians around the world.

The Church of the East

Although other artifacts could serve as examples, the Nestorian Stele provides a useful way to investigate the history of Christianity in Asia by introducing the Church of the East, highlighting Christianity's intermittent existence in Asia, and exploring its precarious relationship with the prevailing culture. Beginning with the first, the earliest groups of Christians in China were part of the Church of the East. In early Christianity, the "one, holy, catholic, and apostolic church" eventually formed into four clusters of churches. These four traditions later came to be called the Catholic Church, the Church of the East, the Eastern Orthodox Church, and the Oriental Orthodox Church (see table 7.1). While the previous chapter discussed the Eastern Orthodox Church, as well as its break with the Oriental Orthodox Church and the Church of the East, this chapter will focus on the Church of the East in more detail.

Of the four clusters of early Christian traditions, the Church of the East had the largest number of believers during the first Christian millennium. Similarly, it "achieved the greatest geographical scope of any Christian church until the Middle Ages."[8] In fact, Asia, which fell under the geographic purview of the Church of the East, "was still home to at least a third of the world's Christians"[9] at the turn of the second millennium. The Church of the East was inherently missional. It sent missionaries and established dioceses all across the continent of Asia—to places like modern Afghanistan, India, Iran, Mongolia, Pakistan, Tibet, Turkmenistan, Uzbekistan, Yemen, and, of course, China. Although these regions lay claim to small populations of Christians today, discoveries of Christian

Table 7.1 Four Early Christian Church Traditions That Widened over Time

Tradition	General Region	Dominant Language Base	Christology
(Roman) Catholic Church	Western and Northern Europe	Latin	Jesus has two natures: human and divine ones that are fully united yet not mixed or divided
Church of the East	Asia and Middle East	Syriac	Jesus has two natures: human and divine ones that are loosely united
Eastern Orthodox	Middle East and Eastern Europe	Greek	Jesus has two natures: human and divine ones that are fully united yet not mixed or divided
Oriental Orthodox	Northern and Eastern Africa and Middle East	Coptic and Armenian	Jesus has one nature after the incarnation: a human and divine one

baptisteries, cemeteries, coins, crosses, churches, inscriptions, murals, and textual fragments demonstrate how thoroughly the Church of the East penetrated these lands.

The Church of the East found its origins in the magi who came from Persia in the Gospel of Matthew. Not surprisingly, it established its headquarters in "the cradle of civilization" along the Tigris and Euphrates Rivers in Seleucia-Ctesiphon by the fifth century and then to nearby Baghdad, Iraq, in the eighth century. There it enjoyed privileged status among the Muslim rulers. The Muslims, in fact, regarded the Church of the East as the ecclesiastical head of world Christianity. Unlike other, more familiar clusters of churches, the Church of the East developed outside of the Byzantine-Roman Empire. It was a minority religion everywhere it existed—always in

Technically, the Byzantine Empire was the eastern remnant of the Roman Empire. However, historians have conveniently used the terms *Byzantine Empire* to refer to the Eastern Roman Empire, headquartered in Byzantium/Constantinople, from 330 to 1453 CE.

religious competition with Buddhism, Confucianism, Hinduism, Islam, Shamanism, or Zoroastrianism. Although it shared essential doctrine with other major Christian bodies, it differed in nonessential matters of theology and practice. For example, the Church of the East did not venerate icons or crucifixes to the same degree as the Eastern Orthodox or Catholic Churches. It also maintained a more optimistic view of humanity and did not develop the doctrine of original sin as formulated in the West.

The Church of the East's liturgical language was Syriac. Hence it naturally drew from the well of Semitic thought, rather than from Greek or Roman thought. Perhaps its Semitic influence is what led it to interpret the union of Jesus' divinity and humanity in a way that differed from the Catholic and Eastern Orthodox traditions in the Byzantine-Roman Empire. Whatever the case, by the end of the fifth century, the Catholic and Eastern Orthodox Churches began labeling the Church of the East "Nestorians" (and thus heretical) under the mistaken notion that the latter had adopted the Christology of Nestorius, bishop of Constantinople from 428 to 431.[10] Despite this division, however, the Church of the East grew under the authority of capable leaders. Patriarch (or Catholicos) Timothy I (r. 780–823), for instance, presided over perhaps "a quarter of the world's Christians."[11]

The On-Again, Off-Again Church

As impressive and encompassing as the church was in Asia, it was not able to sustain its amazing growth. The wave of Christianity rolled onto Asia a few times before surrounding the continent—and even then, its success has been marginal there relative to other parts of the world. The first wave of Christianity splashed onto Asia in the first century and onto China in the seventh century. As mentioned already, the Church of the East was the most widespread and largest body of Christians in Asia during most of the church's past. Despite its astonishing growth and expansion for more than a thousand years, however, it entered several centuries of decline beginning around the turn of the second millennium due to conversions to Islam,

---

 To learn more about the early history of the Church of the East, see Philip Jenkins's *The Lost History of Christianity: The Thousand-Year Golden Age of the Church in the Middle East, Africa, and Asia—and How It Died.*

---

violence and persecution it endured from the state and from overly zealous rulers, pressure from local religions, plagues and agricultural failures, and an inability to connect with changing societies.

The second wave of Christianity entered Asia as the Church of the East embarked on a journey of decline. The first major contact the Catholic Church made with Asia occurred during the Crusades (1095–1291). The collision between the Catholic Church and the Church of the East was both inevitable and lamentable. Both traditions, though united in their commitments to the Nicene Creed, emphasized their differences rather than their similarities—a regular theme in the history of Christianity that we discussed in previous chapters. Notwithstanding the Church of the East's longstanding presence in Asia, the Catholic Church regarded its Asian counterpart as heretical and thus failed to acknowledge its sphere of influence over the continent. The Italian Catholic bishop of Beijing, John of Montecorvino (1247–1328), for instance, converted to Catholicism thousands in China who had formerly belonged to the Church of the East. Later, in the early 1500s, the Catholic Church forced the Christians in India to convert to Catholicism. This dispute caused a church split in the Church of the East that persists to this day. Around this same time period, the Catholic Church began expanding into many regions of Asia where the Church of the East had not existed or where it had vanished. In Southeast Asia, for instance, the Catholic Church witnessed the conversion of most of the inhabitants of the Philippines as well as many in Indonesia and Vietnam. In the meantime, the tide of the Church of the East was ebbing, and the priesthood became hereditary in order to survive.

The last major wave entering Asia was that of Protestant missionaries from the eighteenth through the early twentieth centuries. Although Protestant merchants had resided and traded in Asia since the 1600s through the auspices of businesses like the British East India Company and Dutch East India Company, missions were delayed out of fear that they could disrupt business. Before long, however, Protestant communities were planted and nurtured across Asian cities and distant villages. William Carey (1761–1834) and Amy Carmichael (1867–1951) in India, Robert Morrison (1782–1834) and Hudson Taylor (1832–1905) in China, Horace Allen (1858–1932) and Henry Appenzeller (1858–1902) in Korea, and Adoniram Judson (1788–1850) in Myanmar top the list of some of the best-known Protestant missionaries to Asia, but countless other missionaries and indigenous Christians shaped the development of Asian Protestantism.

Even though no Asian country has come close to embracing Protestant Christianity as its primary religion, Protestant (Western) culture has influenced the region extensively. Protestants advanced the fields of medicine, health care, technology, and education. Protestants built lasting institutions and also pioneered biblical translations. In terms of churches and percentages of Christians, Protestantism has experienced the most success in South Korea and Singapore as well as parts of China. At the same time, its growth has been hampered by Protestant divisions, its general "foreignness," and anti-Western policies in countries such as China, Japan, North Korea, and North Vietnam that have cast a shadow over Christianity.

The Collision between Eastern and Western Worldviews

The last way the Nestorian Stele illumines Christianity in Asia is by raising the issue of contextualization—that is, how to convey the Christian message in a particular context. Despite the fact the Christian faith originated in the Middle East, missionaries from the West struggled consistently with communicating Christianity to an Eastern audience whose customs differed drastically from their own. Given our previous discussion of apostolicity that builds on the thought of the fifth-century French monk Vincent of Lérins, we could phrase the struggle as follows: At what point did Western Christians believe the seed of Christianity "altered" rather than "progressed"? Depending on the group questioned, different answers would have been given.

In India, the Church of the East integrated itself fully into the prevailing Hindu society and caste system, while later Catholic missionaries demonized the Church of the East as idolaters. As for the origin of Christianity in seventh-century China, the Nestorian Stele and contemporary documents found in the Dunhuang cave expressed Christian concepts in Buddhist and Daoist terminology. As one of the scrolls from the cave states:

> As a lamb goes silently to be slaughtered so [the Messiah] was silent, not proclaiming what he had done, for he had to bear in his body the punishment of the Law. Out of love he suffered so that what Adam had caused should be changed by this. While his Five Attributes passed away, he did not die but was released again after his death. Thus it is possible for even those who fail to live after death. Through the holy wonders of the Messiah all can escape becoming ghosts. All of us are saved by his works. You don't need to strengthen to receive him, but he will not leave you weak and vulnerable, without qi [Life Breath, a term used constantly in Daoism].[12]

To the chagrin of some, these writings pushed the limits of Christian theology. They were clearly an "alteration" of the Christian faith. For others, however, they succeeded in articulating the essentials of the Christian faith in culturally appropriate ways. They reflected appropriate growth and "progression" of the Christian seed.

Though unrelated by tradition and by time, the nuanced faith of the Church of the East resembled the accommodationist policies of the Jesuit order of the Catholic Church in many ways. Jesuit missionaries like Matteo Ricci (1552–1610) in China, Francis Xavier (1506–1552) and Robert de Nobili (1577–1656) in India, and Alexander de Rhodes (1591–1660) in Indochina adopted the customs of the cultures in which they resided. Matteo Ricci, for instance, argued that the Chinese classics of Confucianism spoke of the Christian God, while Robert de Nobili copied the habits of Hindu holy men. Scandalously, he wore the garments of a high-caste Brahmin priest and adopted vegetarianism. Rival orders within the Catholic Church such as the Dominicans and Franciscans responded that the Jesuits compromised Christianity's distinctives—sparking what historians later called the Chinese Rites Controversy.

In addition to the struggles of the Catholic Church, Protestants also faced great challenges while attempting to spread Christianity. The Javanese evangelist Kyai Sadrach (1835–1924), for example, diverged from the practices of (Western) missionaries to Indonesia by conducting Christian services that paralleled Muslim ones. He built a church in the style of Javanese mosques and adopted many Javanese Muslim practices. In nearby China, British missionary Hudson Taylor dyed his hair, donned Chinese garments, and grew a beard and ponytail. Many missionaries regarded Taylor's habits as shameful, under the conviction that he was capitulating to heathenism. From our viewpoint, however, we can see how these critics simply drew the line of apostolicity in different places than Hudson did.

Whatever our perspective, there was a sense in which East-West tensions continued mounting in East Asian nations such as China and Japan. It became just as difficult for missionaries to distinguish between culture and gospel as it was for Asian governments to distinguish between Western

---

In this rebellion, the "boxers" were pro-nationalist and anti-imperialist Chinese men intent on removing Western powers from society. It took the militaries of several Western nations like Britain, France, and the United States to suppress the uprising and ensure the safety of Westerners, such as missionaries, living in China.

---

missionaries dedicated to the saving of souls and Western merchants intent on becoming rich no matter the cost. The Taiping Rebellion (1859–1864), for instance, occurred after a Protestant Chinese convert claimed to be the younger brother of Jesus Christ. Many Protestant missionaries originally supported the rebellion, and upwards of twenty million Chinese died. Four decades later, the Boxer Uprising (1899–1901) led to the brutal death of tens of thousands of Chinese Christians and hundreds of missionaries. Increasingly in the twentieth century, there was a movement toward Asian Christians taking the reins of the church. Although this did not fully resolve the challenges of communicating Christianity to an Asian context, it did relax part of the tension and cultural misunderstandings that accompanied the arrival of Western missionaries into a foreign context.

Conclusion: Christianity in a Museum?

In the future, Asian Christianity, like all forms of the Christian faith, will continue to wrestle with questions of oneness and apostolicity. As Christianity has rolled onto Asia over the centuries, one tradition at a time, the different groups of Christians have formed non-connecting streams across the continent. Each group of churches struggles to understand itself as part of the one body of Christ, given its clear differences in temperament and theology from other groups. Of these different traditions struggling to survive, the oldest and smallest of these in Asia is the Church of the East. Although the Nestorian Stele stands as a lasting testimony of its presence and success as the largest Christian body for centuries, the tradition has barely survived the ravages of time, persecution, and disparagement. Even today, the Church of the East struggles to stay live amidst the radical and violent aggression of Muslim extremists.

The stele that proclaims its grandeur in China was discovered by mistake in the seventeenth century under the gaze of a Buddhist monastery. Since 1907, the Nestorian Stele has resided in the Forest of Stone Steles in Xian, China. It was moved into the museum after a Danish adventurer sought to take it to Christian Europe, where it would have presumably found a more welcoming reception after years of having no home. There it modestly stands among several thousand steles resembling it in appearance and design yet paling in comparison to the unrivaled story it tells of a once-thriving community of Christians living in the golden age of Tang China.

 Questions for Personal Exploration

1. Why do you think Christianity all but died out in the Middle Ages in China? What do you think it would take for Christianity to die out in America?

2. Go back and read through each of the longer quotes from primary literature in this chapter. What is the sense you get as you read through them?

3. If you were moving to Asia as a Christian missionary, what would be your first priorities? What cultural challenges do you think you would encounter? How would you deal with them?
4. How do you think you might feel if you lived in a non-Christian country that suddenly began receiving waves of different Christian traditions that did not get along with each other? What would you think of this new and strange religion?

 ## Resources for Deeper Exploration

Baum, Wilhelm, and Dietmar Winkler. *The Church of the East: A Concise History.* London: Routledge, 2003.

Baumer, Christopher. *The Church of the East: An Illustrated History of Assyrian Christianity.* London: I. B. Tauris, 2006.

Bays, David. *A New History of China.* Oxford: Wiley-Blackwell, 2011.

Jenkins, Philip. *The Lost History of Christianity: The Thousand-Year Golden Age of the Church in the Middle East, Africa, and Asia—and How It Died.* New York: HarperOne, 2008.

Keevak, Michael. *The Story of a Stele: China's Nestorian Monument and Its Reception in the West, 1625–1916.* Hong Kong: Hong Kong University Press, 2008.

Palmer, Martin. *The Jesus Sutras: Rediscovering the Lost Scrolls of Taoist Christianity.* New York: Ballantine Wellspring, 2001.

Phan, Peter, ed. *Christianities in Asia.* Oxford: Wiley-Blackwell, 2011.

Wilmshurst, David. *The Martyred Church: A History of the Church of the East.* Sawbridgeworth, Hertfordshire: East & West Publishing, 2011.

 ## Notes

1. Martin Palmer, *The Jesus Sutras: Rediscovering the Lost Scrolls of Taoist Christianity* (New York: Ballantine Wellspring, 2001), 224.

2. Ibid., 227.

3. To read from or about these Christian documents, see ibid.; Ray Riegert and Thomas Moore, eds., *The Lost Sutras of Jesus: Unlocking the Ancient Wisdom of the Xian Monks* (Berkeley, CA: Ulysses, 2006).

4. Christopher Baumer, *The Church of the East: An Illustrated History of Assyrian Christianity* (London: I. B. Tauris, 2006), 166.

5. Ibid., 186.

6. Samuel Moffett, *A History of Christianity in Asia*, vol. 1, *Beginnings to 1500*, 2nd ed. (Maryknoll, NY: Orbis, 1998), 314.

7. Ibid., 1:314.

8. Wilhelm Baum and Dietmar Winkler, *The Church of the East: A Concise History* (London: Routledge, 2003), 1.

9. Philip Jenkins, *The Lost History of Christianity: The Thousand-Year Golden Age of the Church in the Middle East, Africa, and Asia—and How It Died* (New York: HarperOne, 2008), 4.

10. For more on this topic, see Sebastian Brock, "The 'Nestorian' Church: A Lamentable Misnomer," *Bulletin of the John Rylands University Library of Manchester* 3, no. 78 (1996): 23–35.

11. Jenkins, *The Lost History of Christianity*, 6.

12. Palmer, *The Jesus Sutras*, 63.

Fig. 8.1 Early seventeenth-century, copper-alloy cast crucifix from the Kingdom of Kongo. Two figures atop Jesus and one below him, all in prayer. Photo: Brooklyn Museum. CCA-3.0 Unported licence (Wikimedia Commons).

Chapter 8

A Crucifix in the DRC Illumines the History of Christianity in Africa

I t was the 1600s. After obtaining the extracted metal from the ore that a miner had dug in the earth, the African metallurgist began making art from the copper alloy. Before the arrival of the Portuguese in the 1480s, Kongolese metallurgists had made sculptures and other objects for adoration. But everything changed in the year 1491. That's the year the king converted to Christianity. Thereafter, the king ordered the destruction of local temples as well as physical symbols connected to paganism. Such pagan artifacts, he decreed, were to be replaced by large public crosses throughout the kingdom in imitation of the Portuguese Catholics who had erected crosses all throughout the African continent under the bold presupposition that this new land now belonged to the Kingdom of Portugal. It did not take long before portable crosses and crucifixes (crosses affixed with Jesus) also became commonplace in Africa. Using the European crucifix as an example, the skilled Kongolese metallurgist easily adapted the sacred object to local taste by adding African touches to the iconic scene of the Christian story: Jesus dying on a cross for the sins of the world. Within no time, the metallurgist was making dozens of copper alloy crucifixes that measured a few inches to a couple of feet in length. A new form of Christian spirituality in Africa had been born.

The Story of a Crucifix

The art of lost-wax casting was one of the most ancient ways of forming alloy metals such as brass and bronze sculptures.[1] The first use of bronze several thousand years before Christ, during the so-called Bronze Age, allowed ancient civilizations to create objects that withstood the test of time better than other artifacts such as wooden or clay sculptures, paintings, or writings. Today, museums all over the world house metal sculptures and statues coming from long-forgotten cultures and civilizations. In Africa,

The Kingdom of Kongo was an ancient civilization that came to an end in the first two decades of the twentieth century. In parts of the ancient kingdom, two countries with the name "Congo" (spelled with Cs) exist: the Democratic Republic of the Congo (the DRC) and the Republic of the Congo (also known as Congo). The use of the letter K in this chapter always refers to the ancient Kingdom of Kongo and its inhabitants.

cast copper alloy objects date to around the turn of the first Christian millennium. The use of copper alloy probably increased with the arrival of Europeans into Africa in the fifteenth century, since they brought brass and copper. From the seventeenth and eighteenth centuries, in particular, we have many crucifixes made of copper alloy that enhance our understanding of Christianity in the Kingdom of Kongo. In an excavation of a Kongolese church and cemetery in use during the seventeenth and eighteenth centuries, two European scholars discovered hundreds of Christian artifacts, including a couple of Kongolese crucifixes.

The crucifixes they found bore striking resemblances to many others dating from this time period and region. The hands and feet of Christ in Kongolese crucifixes are flattened out according to the style of contemporary Central African art, possibly emphasizing spiritual power. Also, Christ is surrounded by different figures. In some, the Virgin Mary is below his feet, a feature that dates the crucifix to the time period after Capuchin priests arrived. Besides the image of Mary, there are additional saints, angels, or possibly mourners atop Jesus' nailed hands and/or atop his head. This provides the effect of a cosmogram, which predated the arrival of Christians. Christ sometimes has bulging eyes that may symbolize supernatural vision as well as noticeable African facial features and hair. Finally, the Kongolese expanded their use of the crucifix. This included use for enthroning a chief, making judicial decisions, warding off evil spirits, channeling supernatural power, rainmaking and ensuring success in hunting, fighting, traveling, giving birth, and for healing disease.

The Church in Africa

In addition to their use in the Kingdom of Kongo, brass and bronze crucifixes and crosses exist across Africa in Egypt, Ethiopia, and below the Sahara. Such crucifixes shed light on the history of Christianity in Africa by highlighting the pervasive influence of Christianity on the continent as well as clashes that ensued between African and European Christians. In this chapter, we will consider how an African crucifix helps us better understand African Christianity. We will begin our discussion by introducing distinct yet slightly overlapping phases of Christianity in Africa: the early phase, which lasted the first thousand years of Christianity; the second phase, which lasted from about the 1400s to the 1900s; and the most

Egypt and Ethiopia are good examples of regions that have distinct crosses with designs that preceded the arrival of Western missionaries. In Egypt, the cross comes from the ancient Egyptian symbol of the ankh, representing eternal life. In Ethiopia, the cross is typically made from lattice work and is flat with a square at the base representing the famed Ark of the Covenant, rumored to reside in Aksum, Ethiopia.

recent phase, which is about two centuries old. Each phase shaped African Christianity in a profound yet different way. The classification of African Christianity into these different phases is not meant to be exhaustive but rather to illumine the general history of this region.

First Phase of African Christianity: First to Tenth Centuries

The first phase of Christianity dates to the first decade or two after the resurrection of Jesus Christ. The collective memory of Africa attributes the genesis of the church with the arrival of John Mark, the author of the Gospel of Mark, in Alexandria. The Coptic Orthodox Church credits John Mark as the first patriarch. He leads the way in an unbroken chain of more than one hundred patriarchs over more than nineteen hundred years. The church in Egypt played a decisive role in the development of the Christian tradition. It was in Alexandria, for instance, that the first Christian school likely came into existence. Some of the most noteworthy early Christian theologians, such as Clement (d. 215) and Origen (d. 254), were teachers there. Also out of Egypt, we find Alexandria's most famous early patriarch, Athanasius (d. 373), who was significant in the defense of the full divinity of Christ during and after the first Ecumenical Council.

From its arrival and early development in Egypt, Christianity spread southward and eastward into the modern countries of Ethiopia, Eritrea, and Sudan. The Kingdom of Aksum, headquartered in modern Ethiopia, was a Christian empire by the fourth century. Due to an ancient tradition holding that the Ethiopian leaders descended from the kings of Israel (through the union of King Solomon and the Queen of Sheba in the tenth century BCE), Ethiopians practiced a Jewish form of Christianity that celebrated two Sabbaths and placed replicas of the Ark of the Covenant—the original of which is believed to reside in Saint Mary's Cathedral in Aksum, Ethiopia—into all of its churches. The Christians in Ethiopia, as in nearby Sudan, made colorful frescoes on their churches, practiced monasticism, and fell under the jurisdiction of the Coptic Orthodox Church.

On the other side of the continent, in northwestern Africa, an area called the Maghreb by Muslims, the Christianity that emerged shared closer ties with the Catholic Church. We do not have any firm evidence of Christianity entering this region until the second century, but it is likely that it existed before. Whatever the case, Christianity in northwestern Africa experienced great trials in its early years. Up until the fourth century, the Roman Empire persecuted Christians. The most important city in the area was Carthage (near Tunis, Tunisia). At the beginning of the third century, a young Christian noblewoman named Perpetua (d. 203), who was nursing an infant son, was martyred there along with her slave girl Felicitas and several other Christians. In fact, persecution of the church endured for so long in northwestern Africa that a division emerged between those who were more lax and those who were more rigorous in the rehabilitation of those who had abandoned their faith during bursts of persecution. Even well after the time of Augustine (d. 430), the bishop of Hippo (now Annaba, Algeria) who influenced the development of Western Christianity for more than a millennium, disputes lingered between divided Christians in northwestern Africa. What effectively ended the disputes was the rise and expansion of Islam in North Africa beginning in the seventh century, which halted and eventually supplanted Christianity in all of the places where it had formerly thrived in Africa.

Second Phase of African Christianity: Fifteenth to Twentieth Centuries

The second phase of Christianity in Africa lasted from about the fifteenth to the twentieth centuries. It mostly affected sub-Saharan Africa, since Islam dominated the religious landscape of North Africa. The arrival of the Portuguese in the Kingdom of Kongo in the 1480s formed a trading partnership as well as a spiritual alliance. In 1491, the *manikongo*, or ruler, of the kingdom, Nzinga Nkuwu (d. 1509), was baptized into the Catholic Church as João I along with his family. Although he eventually ceased practicing his Christian faith, his son, who was called by his baptismal name Afonso (r. 1509–1542), devoted himself firmly to the adoption of Christianity in his kingdom and the removal of traditional religious practices.

Due to the long reign of Afonso as *manikongo*, the Kingdom of Kongo became a Christian state that fused together Western Catholic and African religious traditional customs. The Portuguese sought to Christianize the

 The so-called Trans-Atlantic Slave Trade, in operation from the fifteenth to the nineteenth centuries, led to the exportation of countless millions of Africans to the Americas and the Caribbean.

people of Kongo, but "both the slave trade and colonization combined to stunt the vigor of evangelization."[2] Although slavery had been part of African culture for some time, the Portuguese increased the demand for slaves. "Chief among those involved in the slave trade were the Catholic clergy, who openly participated in the slave system."[3] Within a few decades, Europeans Christians were purchasing and selling thousands of Africans annually. A letter that Afonso wrote to the king of Portugal in November 1514, for instance, attests to the bad example some of the Portuguese priests were displaying among the Kongolese:

> [Some of the Portuguese priests] moved into separate huts and there welcomed the young people for instruction. They came daily and begged us for money. As we gave them some, they all began to trade—to buy and to sell [slaves]. In view of this disorder we asked them, for the sake of the love of our Lord's will, [at least] to buy only true slaves and above all to buy no

women, in order not to set a bad example and not to represent us as liars in the eyes of the people to whom we had preached. Without bothering themselves about that, they began to fill their houses with women of ill repute. Father Pedro Fernandez took a woman into his house who bore him a mixed-race child. For this reason, the young people who he taught and sheltered in his house fled and told their parents and relatives of the situation. All began then to mock and to laugh at us. They said that all things were probably lies, and that we had deceived them for our own reasons and for white objectives. We were very saddened and did not know how we should respond.[4]

As time passed, the Kongolese king continued to send letters to the Portuguese crown to no avail. The slave trade only grew. Meanwhile, Catholic orders such as the Augustinians, Dominicans, Capuchins, Carmelites, Franciscans, and Jesuits continued to evangelize the local people. The translation of a Catholic catechism into the local language of Kikongo was set to music so that the people could memorize it. Local lay catechists called *maestri* (or "teachers") taught the people the basics of the Christian faith while priests administered sacraments such as baptism, the Eucharist, and last rites.

The Christian traditions that Westerners brought to Africa were Catholicism and Protestantism. These two traditions include the so-called mainline churches founded by European Protestant missionaries, such as Anglicans, Baptists, Methodists, Lutherans, and Presbyterians. These Christian traditions have had to compete not only among themselves but also with African traditional religions and Islam. Taken as a whole, the northern and eastern coasts of Africa are majority Muslim areas; the western and central portions contain high numbers of practitioners of African traditional religions; and the southern part boasts the largest percentages of Christians. At the same time, despite larger commonalities, all countries in these regions possess their own histories that lead them down a certain religious path.

Third Phase of African Christianity: Nineteenth through Twenty-First Centuries

The last phase of the history of Christianity in Africa has been during the last two centuries. In the late nineteenth century, Europeans of all theological and ethnic-national stripes descended on Africa. The period of colonization, which has been called the "Scramble for Africa," dramatically changed the economic, political, and religious landscape of Africa. While Africans were under colonial rule, Western missionaries evangelized, established churches, created schools, and made advances in farming, hygiene, education, and infrastructure. Inevitably, European colonization meant that Europeans maintained control of the Christian churches in Africa. They were slow to concede leadership to locals.

From around the early 1900s, we begin to get our first glimpses of indigenous Africans evangelizing other Africans independently of European oversight. The Liberian prophet William Wade Harris (d. 1929), for instance, was one of the early prophetic leaders of African Christianity whose work was cut short by European governorship. Prior to an evangelistic trip he made around the coast of West Africa, almost a century of Catholic and Protestant missionary work by Westerners in the Ivory Coast had produced a few hundred converts. However, within a few years of Harris's trip, "estimates of Christians in that area ranged between two and three hundred thousand."[5] What accounts for this incredible growth of Christianity? While in prison as an adult, Harris had a vision that would change his life. The year was 1910. According to Harris, the archangel Gabriel visited him in his cell and ordered him to burn the pre-Christian physical objects used for worship (called fetishes), abandon wearing Western clothes, make a long cane for his journeys, adopt other local African customs, and go preach the gospel as if he were a prophet like Elijah or Ezekiel. Harris wore a long white gown, went barefoot, walked with a long cross, and carried a bowl for baptizing. He was accompanied by several women, possibly his wives, who sang loudly and assisted him in his work. A century later, at least a couple of hundred thousand Christians in West Africa attend Harrist churches, but his influence was even wider.[6]

Although European powers held Harris in check by arresting him and refusing him entry into the Ivory Coast on many occasions, his ministry was a foreshadowing of things to come. In the second half of the twentieth century, Africa witnessed an exodus of Western political and religious rule. There was now a united drive toward African independence. The emergence of so-called African Initiated (or Independent) Churches (AICs) followed colonial rule. The numbers of AICs swell into the thousands and claim members into the tens of millions. Many of those in AICs fumed over the second-class treatment they had received during European colonization. Such criticism can be seen in the words of the "founding father" of Kenya, President Jomo Kenyatta (d. 1978), who attended a European-run missionary school:

> We can see . . . that the early teachers of the Christian religion in Africa did not take into account the differences between the individualistic aspects embodied in Christian religion, and the communal life of the African regulated by customs and tradition handed down from generation to generation. They failed, too, to realize that the welfare of the tribes depended on the rigid observance of these tribal taboos and rights, through which all the members of a tribe, from kings and chiefs down to the lowest and most insignificant individual, were bound up as one organic whole and controlled by an iron-bound code of duties. . . . They condemned customs and beliefs which they could not understand. Among other things, the missionary insisted that the followers of the Christian faith must accept monogamy as the foundation of the true Christian religion, and give up the dances, ceremonies and feasts which are fundamental principles of the African social structure.[7]

Whereas Western missionaries tended to stress Western customs such as monogamy; frown upon mixing religion with politics; downplay miracles, divine healing, deliverance ministries, revelatory dreams, and communication with dead ancestors; and limit emotional responses during worship services, AICs embraced these types of practices. The supernatural work of God became a distinct mark not only of Protestant and Pentecostal AICs but also of Catholic ones. In numbers that have been quoted often but still demand repeating, the number of Christians in Africa has increased from roughly ten million in 1900 to a number soon approaching five hundred million.[8] Much of this growth stems from the active evangelistic efforts and ministries of African Initiated Churches of the past century, though other sociological factors such as high birth rates contribute.

Since the late 1900s, there has been an emergence of Pentecostal churches that emphasize wealth and prosperity more than divine healing and exorcisms. They are often based in cities, attract younger and more educated audiences, and offer "emotional, enthusiastic and loud"[9] worship services. These new churches share many commonalities with global Pentecostalism and are not as distinctly African as AICs. Today, they are found throughout Africa in great numbers—for example, the Church of God

International in Benin, the Full Gospel Believers Church in Ethiopia, the Church of Pentecost in Ghana, the Deeper Life Bible Church in Nigeria, and the Zimbabwe Assemblies of God Africa churches in Zimbabwe.

Cultural Clashes between African and European Christians

The distinctions between European-initiated churches and AICs give testimony to the larger cultural differences between Europeans and Africans. Just as African Christians adapted the European crucifix to their own customs and preferences, so they transformed other forms of Christian expression in accordance with their distinct contexts. Naturally, such adaptation provoked criticism from Western missionaries, who regarded different adaptations as "alterations" of the seed of the gospel rather than "progress." In this section, we will look at two cultural clashes between European and African Christians: rainmaking and polygamy. In both instances, we will examine the lives of two famous Christians whose church fellowship and friendship ended due to their contrasting views on these two issues.

The two men I am referring to are David Livingstone (1813–1873) and King Sechele (1831–1892). Dr. David Livingstone was a Scottish missionary who paved the way for future missionary endeavors due to his pioneering treks through the African interior as well as his publications appearing in the West. Sechele, by contrast, was a local king of the Bakwain (or Bakwena) people of modern Botswana, who is less familiar to Western audiences. The two met in 1847. Sechele soon welcomed the strange Westerner and learned from him how to read the Bible and write letters. Their friendship grew strong, and Sechele was making great progress in his faith, but Livingstone was unwilling to baptize the king due to his participation in rainmaking ceremonies and his marriage to five women.

Polygamy and rainmaking were time-honored and socially accepted practices in Africa. Both were connected to kingship, since multiple wives indicated wealth, high status, and respect, while the ability to spiritually generate rain was one of the duties of a king for his people. To get baptized by Livingstone, Sechele was forced to renounce both of these ancient customs. It was a tough decision. Writing in 1858—the year Livingstone reluctantly baptized the king—the missionary penned that Sechele "often assured me that he found it more difficult to give up his faith in [rainmaking] than anything else which Christianity required him to abjure."

Livingstone, by contrast, countered that the only way to guarantee rain was to move close to a "never-failing river, make a canal, and irrigate the adjacent lands."[10] Dancing for rain was pointless, he reasoned.

The difference in thought between these men could not be more apparent. Here we may depict Livingstone as the quintessential Western rationalist and pragmatist, and Sechele as an African diviner who recognized the dynamic relationship between the spiritual and physical worlds. Ironically, the year Livingstone arrived among the Bakwain people, a three-year drought ensued. Despite pleas among the people for Livingstone to allow Sechele to intercede as a rainmaker, the missionary did not relent. Meanwhile, out of deference to his people and in compliance with his duty as a local king, Sechele secretly paid for a rainmaker. Things, however, were about to get worse between missionary and king.

Before long, one of Sechele's former wives became pregnant, thus cutting the bond of peace between Livingstone and Sechele. Polygamy, as already mentioned, was a common feature of African society, and one of the obligations of a husband was to impregnate his wife. Unlike in the West, polygamy was regarded as socially beneficial in Africa, since it permitted the marriage of all women in a society where more females than males made it to adulthood; it allowed men to engage in sexual intercourse, since many tribal groups prohibited intercourse with menstruating, pregnant, or lactating women; and it maintained population control, since polygamous households have fewer children than monogamous ones.[11]

Whatever the perceived social benefits to society, Westerners largely shunned the practice of polygamy, even though African Christians retorted that some of the most prominent figures in the Bible, such as Abraham, Jacob, David, and Solomon, were both polygamists and favored by God. The World Missionary Conference at Edinburgh in 1910, for example,

 There were, of course, some Westerners who made allowance for the practice of polygamy among African Christians, but such missionaries were generally in the minority among Western Christians.

minced no words: Polygamy "is simply one of the gross evils of heathen society, which, like habitual murder or slavery, must at all costs be ended."[12] In the end, Sechele's return to rainmaking and polygamy led his friend and mentor Dr. Livingstone to declare him "an apostate"[13] and false Christian. The two were never reconciled, and Livingstone died in Africa under the weight of never having made one lasting convert, even though Sechele continued to live out his Christian faith from within the context of his African culture.

Conclusion: Lingering Questions

As projections for the future of Christianity in Africa are made, many scholars expect to see continued growth. In fact, before too long, Africa may contain more Christians than any other given part in the world. Despite the incredible growth expected of African Christianity, there will also be many challenges, such as church division, leadership succession, economic and social crises, and religious violence. Some of the lingering questions remaining from our discussion of Christianity in Africa have been summarized as follows by two Western scholars:

> To what extent are received Christian ideas, rituals, and habitual concerns pure and timeless expression of true Christianity?
> To what extent are they merely the preoccupations of the particular people from whom one first learned about Christ?
> To what extent may Africans alter the Christianity they received from Europe without betraying the essence of the faith?[14]

These are challenging questions. What's more, they are just as important to address in Africa as in any other part of the world. Because Westerners have been the predominant carriers of Christianity to other distant cultures, there has been a tendency for Westerners to consider their form of Christianity to be the standard by which all others are judged. Desmond Tutu, the archbishop of Cape Town in South Africa from 1986 to 1996, questioned the privileged position of Western Christian theology many years ago when he wrote, "For too long western theology has wanted to lay claim to a universality that it cannot too easily call its own. Christians have found that the answers they possessed were answers to questions that nobody in different situations was asking. New theologians have arisen, addressing themselves to the issues in front of them [which are very different]."[15]

For some African Christians, theology is not a static form of doctrine that exists in creeds and confessions but a living organism existing in human beings in differing contexts. According to such a mind-set, the truth or legitimacy of Christianity varies from place to place and from person to person. Naturally, such beliefs query the limits of the church's apostolicity and catholicity, but as Christianity in Africa becomes the cutting edge of what God is doing in the world, Western Christians will be forced to ask hard questions about the church's identity and unity in a changing world. Indeed, the many crucifixes found in Western Africa dating from the seventeenth and eighteenth centuries give witness to the fact that Christianity in Africa, though sharing many commonalities with its counterpart in Europe (and elsewhere), will continue to adapt the Christian faith to its unique context.

 ## Questions for Personal Exploration

1. Does Christianity have a "base" in any one geographical location? How does this affect how we understand Christianity?
2. What is the difference between a cross and a crucifix? What would you say to the argument that crucifixes are theologically superior to crosses, since the cross only makes sense if a Savior is dying on it, whereas an empty crucifix potentially leads to a denial of the incarnation? Why do you think Protestant churches typically have crosses while Catholic churches typically have crucifixes?
3. What is the role, if any, of art in Christian churches?
4. Why do you think Christianity suffered almost complete extinction in North Africa during the Middle Ages? How do you think Christianity in North America would respond if it encountered the same threats and challenges?
5. How might the conflict between Livingstone and Sechele play out in today's world? Are there new realities that Christians in Africa face that refute or confirm either side's opinions or actions?

 ## Resources for Deeper Exploration

Bediako, Kwame. *Christianity in Africa: The Renewal of a Non-Western Religion.* Maryknoll, NY: Orbis, 1995.

Fromont, Cecile. *The Art of Conversion: Christian Visual Culture in the Kingdom of Kongo.* Chapel Hill: University of North Carolina Press, 2014.

Isichei, Elizabeth. *A History of Christianity in Africa.* Grand Rapids: Eerdmans, 1995.

Noll, Mark, and Carolyn Nystrom. *Clouds of Witnesses: Christian Voices from Africa and Asia*. Downers Grove, IL: InterVarsity, 2011.

Orobator, Agbonkhianmeghe. *Theology Brewed in an African Pot*. Maryknoll, NY: Orbis, 2008.

Sundkler, Bengt, and Christopher Steed. *A History of the Church in Africa*. Cambridge: Cambridge University Press, 2000.

ᙆ Notes

1. Lost-wax casting "begins by covering a core of clay with a layer of wax. This wax layer is then modeled, carved, and incised by the sculptor to create final surface details. Another layer of clay then encases the wax form and is left to dry. After drying, the clay mold is heated to melt the wax. Molten metal is poured in the clay mold. Once the metal has cooled, the clay mold is broken open, resulting in a unique work." Christa Clarke, *The Art of Africa*, vol. 1, *A Resource for Educators* (New York: Metropolitan Museum of Art, 2006), 36.

2. Ogbu Kalu, "African Christianity: An Overview," in *African Christianity: An African Story*, ed. Ogbu Kalu (Trenton, NJ: Africa World Press, 2007), 24.

3. Ch. Didier Gondola, *The History of Congo* (Westport, CT: Greenwood, 2002), 32.

4. Klaus Koschorke, Frieder Ludwig, Mariano Delgado, and Roland Spliesgart, *A History of Christianity in Asia, Africa and Latin America, 1450–1990: A Documentary Sourcebook* (Grand Rapids: Eerdmans, 2007), 151–52.

5. Mark Noll and Carolyn Nystrom, *Clouds of Witnesses: Christian Voices from Africa and Asia* (Downers Grove, IL: InterVarsity, 2011), 66.

6. Ibid., 78.

7. Quoted in Klaus Koschorke et al., *A History of Christianity*, 242.

8. Dyron Daughrity, *The Changing World of Christianity: The Global History of a Borderless Religion* (New York: Peter Lang, 2010), 193.

9. Allan Anderson, *An Introduction to Pentecostalism: Global Charismatic Christianity* (Cambridge: Cambridge University Press, 2014), 132.

10. David Livingstone, "Conversations in Rain-Making," in *Perspectives on Africa: A Reader in Culture, History and Representation*, ed. Roy Grinker, Stephen C. Lubkemann, and Christopher B. Steiner (Oxford: Wiley-Blackwell, 2010), 245.

11. Ambe Njoh, *Tradition, Culture and Development in Africa: Historical Lessons for Modern Planning* (Aldershot: Ashgate, 2006), 65.

12. Quoted in Adrian Hastings, ed., *The Church in Africa 1450–1950*, Oxford History of the Christian Church (Oxford: Clarendon, 1994), 317.

13. Ibid., 320.

14. Paul Spickard and Kevin Cragg, *A Global History of Christians: How Everyday Believers Experienced Their World* (Grand Rapids: Baker, 1994), 437.

15. John Parrat, *Reinventing Christianity: African Theology Today* (Grand Rapids: Eerdmans, 1995), 2.

Image of Our Lady of Guadalupe in Mexico City's Basilica of Our Lady of Guadalupe. Tomasz Pado, 2007. PHOTO: TOMASZ PADO. CC-BY SA 3.0 UNPORTED LICENSE (WIKIMEDIA COMMONS).

Chapter 9

A Cloak in Mexico Illumines the History of Christianity in Latin America

uauhtlatoatzin, a name that means "eagle that speaks"[1] or "one who talks like an eagle,"[2] lived during the height of the encounter between the Spaniards and the native peoples of Latin America. Like many other villages and people groups, Cuauhtlatoatzin's had recently come under the authority of the mighty Aztec Empire, a kingdom that consisted of an alliance of several tribes. Cuauhtlatoatzin belonged to the largest and lowest-ranking class of Aztec society and made a living by selling crops from his small farm and weaving mats. In 1525, at around the age of fifty, he was baptized into the Catholic Church and received the name Juan Diego. A pious convert, Juan Diego walked fourteen miles every Saturday and Sunday to attend Mass and catechism class.

One Saturday morning in 1531, a voice called Juan Diego's name in his native language. It was the Virgin Mary dressed as a young Aztec princess. She ordered him to build a shrine. Puzzled yet obedient, Juan Diego conveyed the message to the Franciscan bishop, Father Juan de Zumárraga (r. 1530–1548), who listened but would not authenticate the story apart from a sign. The Marian apparition—and Juan Diego's subsequent communication with the bishop—occurred three more times until the humble farmer brought the proof that Father Zumárraga had required. In the dead of winter, Juan Diego carried roses not indigenous to Mexico under his cloak; when he opened his cloak to the bishop, the roses fell to the ground, and the glowing image of the Virgin Mary lay imprinted on the white cloth inside. Convinced of the miracle, the bishop ordered the construction of a shrine on the very spot where the Virgin Mary had been appearing to

Juan Diego. Today, in the back of the Basilica of Our Lady of Guadalupe in Mexico City, an enclosed casing of Juan Diego's cloak with the Virgin Mary's imprint still visible commands the adoration of millions of Catholics around the world.

The Story of a Cloak

The cloak that Juan Diego wore is called a *tilma*. It was a piece of cloth made of agave and other fibers that people commonly wore and used for work and other purposes in Aztec society. The Aztec Empire was a fairly recent one when the Spaniards entered Mexico in 1519. Religion was an essential component of Aztec society. In imitation of the gods that sacrificed themselves in order to bring life into the world, human sacrifice became a regular practice that had reached epic proportions—several thousand sacrifices each year—by the time the Spaniards arrived. After the Spaniards dismantled the capital of the Aztec Empire in the early 1520s, they commissioned missionaries into various regions of Mexico to teach the people about the Christian faith. They prohibited human sacrifice and attempted to draw clear parallels and contrasts between Christianity and the pervasive religious culture of the Aztecs.

In 1524, twelve Franciscan missionaries entered Mexico under the belief that they were preparing the native peoples for the end of the world. Two of

It would not be too much of an exaggeration to state that there have been Christians of every generation since the time of Jesus believing that they were living in "the last days." From Martin of Tours, to Joachim of Fiore, to Melchior Hoffman, to Cotton Mather, and William Miller, countless predictions of the end of the world have come and gone among Christians.

their converts were Juan Diego and his wife. It was several years later, after Juan Diego's baptism and catechesis class, that he first heard the Virgin calling to him in his native language of Nahautl in December 1531. The Virgin Mary had called to him from atop Tepeyac Hill, "a pre-Hispanic Aztec site dedicated to the virgin mother of the gods, Tonantzin."[3] Dressed as a young Aztec princess with a dark complexion, Our Lady spoke as follows:

> Know the Mother of the True God in whom we live, of the Creator in whom all exist, Lord of Heaven and Earth. I

greatly desire that a temple be built [for] me here, that in it I may manifest and give to all my love, pity, help, and defense, for I am your mother, yours and all the dwellers in this land and the others who love me and call upon me and trust in me; here I will listen to their pleas, and remedy their sufferings, griefs, and pains.[4]

After Father Zumárraga came to believe the story several days later, the establishment of a church shrine on this site in central Mexico began in earnest. With ongoing installments, the Old Basilica was completed in 1709. In the late twentieth century, a new basilica was built to house the *tilma*, where it hangs today in a casing under a cross.

The Social Context of Latin America

The proudly displayed *tilma* of Juan Diego illumines the history of Christianity in Latin America by throwing light on the social history of Latin America, showing its esteem of the Virgin Mary, and highlighting its bridge between European and Indian cultures. Beginning with the first, many scholars have emphasized the class struggles between the wealthy and the poor in Latin America by tracing this struggle all the way back to the arrival of the Europeans in the late fifteenth century. Such an understanding contrasts the so-regarded powerless, poor, and native voice of Cuauhtlatoatzin with the powerful, rich, and conquering voice of Spanish-born Bishop Juan de Zumárraga. Whether or not such an interpretation captures the whole story, there is no denying that the Catholic Church of the Old World has played a part in the class struggles of Latin America.

How did this struggle begin? The Iberian empires of Spain and Portugal controlled Latin America for three hundred years. Spain, which began exploration of the region beginning in 1492, divided the area into various administrative divisions whose borders shifted regularly: the Viceroyalty of New Spain (southwestern United States, Mexico, and part of the Caribbean); the Kingdom of Guatemala (Central America), the Viceroyalty of New Granada (northern South America); the Viceroyalty of Peru (Peru and Chile); and the Viceroyalty of Rio de la Plata (southern and central regions of South America). Portugal, for its part, arrived in the Americas in 1500 and maintained Brazil as a viceroyalty as late as 1815. That year, the prince of Portugal, Pedro I "the Liberator" (r. 1822–1831), elevated Brazil to a kingdom alongside Portugal, which it remained until 1822, when Brazil declared independence.

During the colonial period, the Iberians dominated all levels of political, religious, and economic society. For the Iberians, politics and religion formed a knot that could not be untangled. Divided between peninsulars (Europeans born in the Old World) and creoles (Europeans born in the New World), these two European cultures quarreled with one another to the detriment of the local people. The origin of their disputes had to do with the papal-affirmed right of royal "patronage," whereby the pope of the Catholic Church allowed the Spanish and Portuguese crowns to possess the legal entitlement to appoint governmental and religious leaders in their respective colonies. To the chagrin of the land-owning and proud creoles who grew up in the New World and believed they deserved leadership preference, the Spanish and Portuguese crowns usually appointed peninsulars who knew little of the region or the people they governed.

Between 1810 and 1825, most of the countries in Latin America achieved independence. The Napoleonic invasion of the Iberian Peninsula left the Latin American colonies without firm governance from the Old World. In 1808, the French imprisoned the Spanish monarch while the Portuguese monarchy fled to Brazil in anticipation of a similar fate. Despite official freedom from Spain and Portugal, landowning and church-leading

Table 9.1 Historic "Caste System" in Latin America. Although so-called peninsulars and creoles held the majority of power, many other cultural groups came into being with the arrival of the Spanish into Latin America in the late 1400s.

Cultural Group	Description
Peninsular	European born in Old World
Creole	European born in New World
Mestizo	European + Amerindian
Pure	European + Mestizo
Mulatto	European + African
Zambo	Amerindian + African
Amerindian	Indigenous American Indian

creoles still clung tightfisted to power and rarely shared it with local non-European Catholics. After the peninsulars returned to the Old World by 1825, it did not take long before the privileged creoles began fighting with each other and eventually splitting into two distinct yet still elite camps: liberals and conservatives.

The liberals, who were influenced by the French and American revolutions in the late eighteenth century as well as the Enlightenment in general, held as key tenets constitutional liberties such as freedom of speech and assembly, limited (laissez-faire) government, equality before the law, separation of church and state, and religious toleration. This group eventually came to resent the special privileges of the church, with its vast landholdings, obligatory tithes, and great wealth. The conservatives, by contrast, sought to preserve traditional political and religious (Catholic) structures after independence. They descended from the upper class and attempted to stabilize society by reinforcing long-established roles and customs.

The twentieth century proved a pivotal one for Latin American Christianity, as Protestantism, particularly Pentecostalism, Orthodoxy, indigenous religious practices, and secularism have begun to seriously transform the religious landscape. Catholicism, though far from dead, is fast becoming just one religious option for the hundreds of millions who call Latin America home. Liberation Theology, birthed in the 1970s in South America, has changed the face of the Catholic Church to some extent by connecting

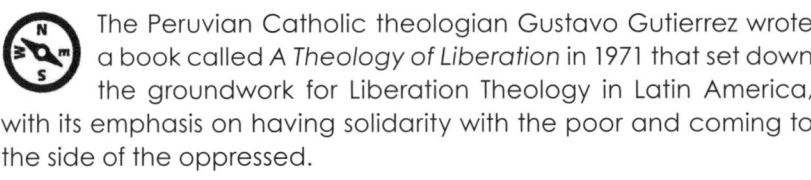

The Peruvian Catholic theologian Gustavo Gutierrez wrote a book called *A Theology of Liberation* in 1971 that set down the groundwork for Liberation Theology in Latin America, with its emphasis on having solidarity with the poor and coming to the side of the oppressed.

to the common person. In the past few decades, for instance, the Catholic Church has sponsored Christian Base Communities (CBCs) and other Catholic social-action groups in order to better instruct laypeople. Yet great challenges lie in store for the Catholic Church as it is forced to compete with Pentecostalism, a branch of Protestant Christianity that has a knack for connecting with the poor and disenfranchised as well as with middle and even upper classes of Latin American society. Since its birth in Latin America in the first decade of the twentieth century, it has stabilized during the past few decades to become a more mainstream option for religious seekers.

Devotion to the Virgin Mary

The second way the *tilma* and tale of Juan Diego throw light on the history of Christianity in Latin America is by underscoring the great devotion that Latin American Catholics give to the Virgin Mary. Whereas Protestantism has tended to diminish the role of Mary in the Christian life, the Orthodox and Catholic traditions have greatly honored her. From a very early time, Christians esteemed her in icons, paintings, and statues. They venerated her in the Roman catacombs of the late first and early second centuries, and an arsenal of early church fathers marshaled reasons for devotion to Mary. She was celebrated as the bridge linking the divine and human as well as the second Eve who played a part in the restoration of humanity to God. A long-standing tradition, summarized in table 9.2, regards her as the Mother of God (Theotokos), conceived apart from original sin (immaculate conception), who never had sexual relations with a man (perpetual virginity) and was translated into heaven at the end of her earthly life (assumption).

The form of piety the Spaniards transplanted into the New World highly regarded the Virgin Mary. They related to Mary in many ways, including as "mother, queen, intercessor, virgin, miracle worker, apocalyptic messenger, the second Eve, handmaiden of God, [and as] heavenly bride."[5] Due to her perceived aid in battle against Muslims, the Spaniards also experienced her as a conqueror—a *conquistadora*. Shrines in honor of Mary dotted the Spanish landscape, just as they did elsewhere across Europe and the Middle

Table 9.2 Four Dogmas of the Virgin Mary

Dogma	Biblical Basis	Official Acceptance	Pronouncement
Mother of God	"The Holy Spirit will come upon you, and the power of the Most High will overshadow you; therefore the child to be born will be holy; he will be called Son of God." (Luke 1:35)	Council of Ephesus (431)	"If anyone does not confess that Emmanuel [Christ] is God in truth, and therefore that the holy virgin is the mother of God (for she bore in a fleshly way the Word of God become flesh), let him be anathema."[a]

Immaculate conception	"I will put enmity between you and the woman, and between your offspring and hers." (Gen. 3:15); "Greetings, favored one! The Lord is with you." (Luke 1:28)	Papal bull *Ineffabilis Deus*, issued in 1854	"We declare, pronounce and define . . . the doctrine which holds that the Most Blessed Virgin Mary, at the first instant of her conception, was preserved immune from all stain of sin, by a singular grace and privilege of the Omnipotent God, in view of the merits of Jesus Christ."[b]
Perpetual virginity	"Mary said to the angel, 'How can this be, since I am a virgin?'" (Luke 1:34)	Lateran Synod in 649	"The blessed ever-virginal and immaculate Mary conceived, without seed, by the Holy Spirit, and without loss of integrity brought Him forth, and after his birth preserved her virginity inviolate."[c]
Assumption	"A great portent appeared in heaven: a woman clothed with the sun, with the moon under her feet, and on her head a crown of twelve stars." (Rev. 12:1)	Papal bull *Munificentissimus Deus*, issued in 1950	"The Immaculate Mother of God, the ever Virgin Mary, having completed the course of her earthly life, was assumed body and soul into heavenly glory."[d]

[a] Quoted in Philip Jenkins, *Jesus Wars: How Four Patriarchs, Three Queens, and Two Emperors Decided What Christians Would Believe for the Next 1,500 Years* (New York: HarperOne, 2010), 165.

[b] Mark Miravelle, *Introduction to Mary: The Heart of Marian Doctrine and Devotion*, rev. ed. (Goleta, CA: Queenship, 2006), 69.

[c] Ibid., 56.

[d] Ibid., 73.

East, and it was not uncommon for Mary to materialize to those who were in need and called for her aid. In a similar way, cults of the Virgin Mary appeared throughout Latin America—for instance, Our Lady of Copacabana in Bolivia, Our Lady of Aparecida in Brazil, Our Lady of the Angels in Costa Rica, and Our Lady of Good Success in Ecuador. From among the Mayas of Central America to the Incas of South America, the Virgin Mary materialized in apparitions, paintings, and statues.

Although many early Protestant leaders affirmed Mary as Mother of God and as ever-virgin, others have removed her from the pedestal of early and medieval church history. Many Protestants feel uncomfortable with the devotion Catholic and Orthodox believers offer her, under the conviction that such veneration has no basis in the Bible and that such veneration ascribes to Mary a status rivaling that of the Trinity. As we discussed in our chapter on apostolicity, the debate could be framed in the following way: Does devotion to Mary represent a "progression" of the Christian faith or an "alteration"? Is it a case of maturation or mutation? For most Protestants, Marian devotion is an alteration garnering no support from Scripture, while for Catholic and Orthodox Christians, devotion to her is a natural development of Christian practice. Using the language of Vincent of Lérins and working from a belief in the twin sources of Scripture and

Part of the disagreement between Catholics and Protestants, for example, has to do with their sources for theology. While Catholics trace their beliefs and practices to the twin sources of Sacred Scripture and Sacred Tradition, Protestants have historically attempted to draw their theology from Scripture alone.

tradition, Catholic theologian Mark Miravelle writes, "Every Church doctrine about the Mother of Jesus has at least an implicit presence in Sacred Scripture, and this scriptural 'seed' is then nurtured and developed under the guidance of the Holy Spirit in the Church's Tradition and history, until it becomes the great 'tree' of a Marian doctrine or dogma."[6]

Whether the form of Marian devotion Catholics display today represents a progression or an alteration of the seed of the gospel is a debate that will not end anytime soon. In the past as today, Christians have to avoid the extremes of making too little and making too much of Mary. While Catholics, in general, criticize Protestants for disregarding the mother of Jesus as an immaterial means to an end (Jesus), Protestants accuse the former of worshiping her as a god.

Bridge between European and Indigenous Cultures

The last way the cloak of Juan Diego illumines the history of Christianity in Latin America is by serving as a bridge between two major cultures. The culture of the Iberians (that is, the Spanish and Portuguese) and that of the indigenous Americans appeared to share little in common. They spoke different languages, practiced different religions, held different customs, and lived in different ways. Needless to say, one of the greatest challenges the Iberian missionaries faced was how to communicate the Christian message to the people they encountered. This was especially difficult given that the Spaniards were systematically erasing the social, political, and religious culture of the people they were conquering.

The Spanish devotion to Mary served as a link with the indigenous people of the Americas who revered various mother goddesses. As already mentioned, the shrines to the Virgin Mary proliferated across Latin America as Catholicism entered these regions. The basis for these shrines was in the Old World. Marian apparitions, in fact, were fairly commonplace. The Virgin Mary was invoked on a daily basis by pious Christians in search of health, wealth, faith, and refuge. As with Our Lady of Guadalupe in Mexico, many Marian shrines in Europe and Asia depicted Mary as dark-skinned, an image referred to as a Black Madonna. One of these in Spain, called Our Lady of Guadalupe, was the origin of the shrine in Mexico—not surprising given that many Spanish conquistadors and settlers originated in that part of Iberia.

While Catholic missionaries were not attempting to eradicate all of the vestiges that remained from the pre-Christian society of the Americas, they sought to draw comparisons between Christian concepts and saints and indigenous ones. The most famous example, the apparition of the Virgin Mary to Juan Diego, was essential to the success of Christianity in Mexico, for it linked the faith of the Spaniards with the faith of the indigenous people. The Virgin Mary appeared to a lowly farmer in his native (Nahuatl) language, dressed as an Aztec princess, and on the holy site of a pre-Christian goddess.

The connections made between foreign and indigenous cultures were not always looked on with favor by missionaries. On a more negative note, a German Jesuit named Joseph Och (1725–1773) wrote disparagingly of the Pima peoples of Mexico: "In their customs the Indians are secretive

toward the missionaries. Even among those who otherwise are good Christians there always clings something of the former odor of impiety."[7] More
positively, however, the Jesuits in Paraguay experienced a great deal of success among the Guarani people. The Jesuits constructed what are called
reductions—missionary towns that brought together the indigenous people
for the purpose of Christian instruction and government. Unlike evangelism elsewhere in the Caribbean and in Latin America, the *reductions* in
Paraguay afforded the local people a way to convert to Christianity without
adopting all of the customs of the Europeans. This was the general approach
of the Jesuit order, which received ample criticism among the many other
Catholic orders for such practices.

Conclusion: What a Difference a Cloak Can Make

Today, more than sixteen million pilgrims and tourists annually visit the
church showcasing the *tilma* of Juan Diego. The national shrine featuring
the *tilma* brings together rich and poor, young and old, believer and skeptic.
Without too much exaggeration, it is the heartbeat of Mexican Christianity.
Undeniably, the basilica housing the cloak is a worldwide site of pilgrimage
among Catholics. Yet the *tilma* of Juan Diego is also one of the most concrete examples of division between the Catholic and Orthodox traditions
and Protestant ones. The latter tradition, sometimes characterized as overly
rational and anti-material, is naturally skeptical of a piece of cloth imprinted
with the image of Mary for the purpose of devotion. Just as one part of the
church, therefore, regards the *tilma* and shrine as a regrettable development
in the history of religion, another one celebrates it as a miracle worthy of
adoration to God. In the end, both traditions seek to honor the customs and
practices passed to them within their constantly changing contexts.

 Questions for Personal Exploration

1. What do you think are the distinctives of Latin American Christianity?
2. Go back and read through each of the longer quotes from primary literature in this chapter. What is the sense you get as you read through them?
3. Why do you think Protestant churches typically pay considerably less
   attention to the Virgin Mary than the Catholic and Orthodox churches do?
4. How do you think you would respond if you were a Protestant pastor

and a parishioner claimed to have had an apparition of the Virgin Mary? How would you pastor him or her through this experience? In a related way, why do you think this type of experience would rarely occur in a Protestant church?

 **Resources for Deeper Exploration**

Anderson, Carl, and Eduardo Chavez. *Our Lady of Guadalupe: Mother of the Civilization of Love*. New York: Doubleday, 2009.

Chasteen, John. *Born in Blood and Fire: A Concise History of Latin America*. 3rd ed. New York: W. W. Norton, 2011.

Gonzalez, Ondina, and Justo Gonzalez. *Christianity in Latin America: A History*. Cambridge: Cambridge University Press, 2007.

Pardo, Osvaldo. *The Origins of Mexican Catholicism: Nahua Rituals and Christian Sacraments in Sixteenth-Century Mexico*. Ann Arbor: University of Michigan Press, 2004.

Pelikan, Jaroslav. *Mary through the Centuries: Her Place in the History of Culture*. New Haven, CT: Yale University Press, 1996.

Rubin, Miri. *Mother of God: A History of the Virgin Mary*. New Haven, CT: Yale University Press, 2009.

Schwaller, John. *The Catholic Church in Latin America: From Conquest to Revolution and Beyond*. New York: New York University Press, 2011.

Notes

1. Carl Anderson and Eduardo Chavez, *Our Lady of Guadalupe: Mother of the Civilization of Love* (New York: Doubleday, 2009), 5.

2. "Juan Diego (1474–1548)," in *The Encyclopedia of Saints*, ed. Rosemary Guiley (New York: Visionary Living, 2001), 194.

3. Ondina Gonzalez and Justo Gonzalez, *Christianity in Latin America: A History* (Cambridge: Cambridge University Press, 2008), 55.

4. "Virgin of Guadalupe," in *Religion in America: A Documentary History*, ed. Lee Penyak and Walter Petry (Maryknoll, NY: Orbis, 2006), 96.

5. Amy Remensnyder, *La Conquistadora: The Virgin Mary and War and Peace in the Old and New Worlds* (Oxford: Oxford University Press, 2014), 8.

6. Mark Miravelle, *Introduction to Mary: The Heart of Marian Doctrine and Devotion*, rev. ed. (Goleta, CA: Queenship, 2006), 10.

7. "A German Jesuit among the 'Savage' Pima," in Penyak and Petry, *Religion in America*, 71.

Fig. 10.1 The Apostolic Faith Gospel Mission on Azusa Street in 1907. Apostolic Faith International Headquarters, Portland, Oregon. Photo: Public domain.

Chapter 10

A Warehouse in California Illumines the History of Christianity in North America

The year was 1906. Los Angeles was a large town by contemporary standards but nothing like the bustling and sprawling metropolis that it is today. It was growing each day, however, as up to three thousand people were arriving monthly to eke out a living in the fastest growing city in the newly engrafted state of California. As scholar Harvey Cox remarks about Los Angeles, "The city was populated by people who came from somewhere else because they were looking for something different."[1] Some of the thousands who entered Los Angeles in the first decade of the twentieth century visited a boxy wooden building that measured forty by sixty feet in a neighborhood mostly populated by African American, Jewish, Russian, and Japanese residents, living among lumberyards and other small businesses.

Those who entered the formerly abandoned warehouse on 312 Azusa Street were met with a green painted sign written in Persian: "Mene, Mene, Tekel, Upharsin" (Dan. 5:25, KJV). Such an enigmatic sign did not bode well for the secular journalists drawn to report on the strange happenings on this site. On April 18, 1906, the *Los Angeles Times* reported that the "company of fanatics" at the "tumble-down shack" breathed "strange utterances" and advanced "weird doctrines."[2] The motley group of people who came congregated in a small room on a dirt floor. The straw and sawdust beaten down into the dirt, the lack of proper insulation, the smell of perspiring bodies, and the swarm of flies indicated the building's former purpose: that of a stable. Nevertheless, as admirers were wont to indicate, such were the birth conditions of Jesus the Messiah, and such were the birth conditions of the worldwide Pentecostal movement.

The Story of a Warehouse

The Azusa Street Revival was most active between 1906 and 1909. It was not the earliest Pentecostal movement in history, but it became the center of North American Pentecostalism and the catalyst for its global expansion. The warehouse-turned-mission in which the Holy Spirit made an abode during those years was being leased for $8 a month before the Apostolic Faith Mission purchased it from First African Methodist Episcopal Church for $15,000. The building had recently housed horses and lumber, so the church needed to be cleaned. Inside the main worship room on the first floor, a wooden makeshift pulpit covered in cotton cloth stood at the center. The whitewashed walls and dirt floors flickered with candlelight. The second floor was divided into several rooms, including a church office, prayer room, and bedroom for William J. Seymour (1877–1922), the church's leader, and his wife Jenny (also spelled Jennie) Evans Moore Seymour (1883–1936), who became the pastor after her husband's death.

William Seymour was the most unlikely of candidates for the inauguration of a global religious movement. Born to former slaves in Louisiana, Seymour was an African American with little schooling, one eye blind from smallpox, and no particular trade. In early adulthood, he traveled throughout the South and Midwest before settling for a time in Houston,

Unlike "Jim Crow" laws, which segregated African Americans in public places in the South, the Azusa Street Revival was intentionally interracial. Blacks and whites sat, sang, and prayed together. In this way, the earliest Pentecostals "vigorously and conspicuously fought segregationist urges, initially developing a pattern of inclusiveness and interracial leadership that had been unprecedented in American religious history."[3]

Texas. There, in 1905, he became acquainted with Charles Parham (1873–1929), a self-taught white Christian teacher and healer under whom the gift of speaking in tongues was ignited at a Bible school he ran in Topeka, Kansas, in 1901. Parham was intent on spreading his theological views and so opened a short-lasting Bible school in Houston. Because of segregation laws in Texas, Seymour was legally unable to attend classes with whites, who comprised the overwhelming majority of students. Parham, however, agreed to allow Seymour to listen from the hallway.

In the winter of 1906, immediately after learning from Parham at the school in Houston, Seymour accepted an invitation from an African American woman named Lucy Farrow to serve at a storefront mission in Los Angeles. After his first sermon, in which he preached that speaking in tongues is the only evidence of baptism of the Holy Spirit (a position he later abandoned), Seymour was locked out of the building. Thereafter, he launched prayer meetings at a home where he was living on North Bonnie Brae Street. In April of that year, he and his followers began speaking in tongues and quickly set their sights on securing a more suitable location after they outgrew the house. The location they chose was 312 Azusa Street. From this most unlikely of places, the fledgling church fanned the flames of God's Spirit. Thousands of people from around the globe—of all colors and ethnicities as well as economic and educational backgrounds—rushed to the destination like spiritual prospectors in search of gold. Seymour held three services every day of the year for more than three years. The journal connected to the church cataloged countless numbers of healings and wonders, and hardly a service transpired where there were not people being slain in the Spirit, being healed of physical ailments, and praising God in unknown tongues.

American Pentecostal Churches

The Azusa Street Revival was one of the most intriguing, if not important, revivals in the history of American Christianity. The events that transpired at this warehouse-turned-mission illumine American Christianity in many ways, for they shed light on Pentecostal Christianity, American revivalism, and the interracial history of American church life. Beginning with the first, Pentecostalism is a marriage of African spirituality and Protestant thought. The African American roots of the Pentecostal movement have long been overlooked, but recent scholarship has shown how foundational African American Christianity was to this movement. As African American Pentecostal historian Estrelda Alexander writes, Pentecostalism draws "from the deep wells of African spirituality, slave religion, the independent black churches that came out of reconstruction and the nineteenth-century black Holiness movement that unfolded among free Methodists and Baptists."[4] White historian of world Christianity Dale Irvin agrees. He wrote that

> there can no longer be any doubt that William J. Seymour and
> the entire Azusa Street Mission and Revival that he led were

fully within the Black Church tradition. Azusa Street was many things, but it was first of all a Black Church. We cannot truly understand or appreciate Pentecostalism as a global Christian phenomenon without understanding its deep (although not exclusive) roots in the African American religious world and in the Black Church tradition, specifically the black Holiness church tradition. . . . Without such an understanding, global Pentecostalism has found itself in an identity crisis.[5]

Due to its pivotal role, it is important to briefly describe the African American roots of Pentecostalism. From the seventeenth century onward, the majority of slaves arriving in America came from the West Coast of Africa. Despite regional cultural, linguistic, and religious differences, they each shared many similarities in terms of belief in a Supreme Being, reverence for ancestors, belief in the spiritual world, a strong communal identity, and a creative synthesis of music, song, and dance during worship. When African slaves embraced Christianity in America, they naturally drew from this rich religious heritage. The Negro Spirituals, dancing, communal identity, oral stories from the Bible, and sensitivity to dreams and the spiritual world were important features of African American Christianity, which also drew from Baptist, Methodist, and Holiness Protestant teachings. The blending of African spirituality with Protestant thought can be seen in the work of black Holiness evangelists such as Amanda Berry Smith (1837–1915, who taught and preached in Liberia, Sierra Leone, India, the United States, and the United Kingdom), as well as Charles Price Jones (1865–1949) and Charles Harrison Mason (1866–1961), who were important Baptist-influenced Holiness leaders during the late nineteenth and early twentieth centuries.

The distinct feature of Holiness churches, whether African American or Caucasian, was its interpretation and development of Englishman John Wesley's (1703–1791) views on sanctification. Wesley argued that salvation consists of what he called two "grand branches, justification and sanctification."[6] Justification restores people to the favor of God, while sanctification restores them to the image of God. Though he did not ignore the doctrine of justification, Wesley did accentuate sanctification. In addition to bringing focus to this doctrine, Wesley also emphasized the role the Holy Spirit plays in the believer's life. Wesley's personal and much-publicized experience with the Spirit's work in his life—the so-called Aldersgate experience on May 24, 1738—confirmed his belief that the

Holy Spirit is directly available to believers. The idea that Wesley's followers embraced and developed most emphatically was his belief in what he called "Christian perfection" or "entire sanctification," when God purifies the heart of a believer, removes (original) sin, and empowers the Christian to live free from sin (but not temptation) for the rest of his or her life. The distillation of this would become the Holiness movement, and a part of this movement would be instrumental in the development of Pentecostalism in both its African American and Caucasian streams.

The leader of the Azusa Street Revival, William Seymour, was deeply influenced by Holiness theology as well as by the African spirituality prevalent in his home state of Louisiana. It is now agreed that Seymour's twin influences of African and European Protestant thought and practice contributed to the unique spirituality of the Azusa Street Revival. In particular, scholars have noted the clear parallels between African religion and Pentecostalism when it comes to harnessing spiritual power, singing, dancing, openness to women leadership, and divine healing.

Following the height of the Azusa Street Revival, Spirit-filled Christians from all parts of the country (and world) returned to their homes and established Pentecostal communities. Multiple denominations and church bodies sprang up across the country. Two prominent Pentecostal leaders were Charles Harrison Mason, mentioned above, and Aimee McPherson (1890–1944). Like Seymour, Mason was a Baptist preacher influenced deeply by African religion and Holiness theology. When revival broke out at Azusa Street, Mason traveled there and experienced baptism of the Holy Spirit. Upon his return home, he broke away from his colleague Charles Price Jones over the issue of Spirit baptism. After Mason took sole leadership of the Church of God in Christ (COGIC) in Memphis, Tennessee, Price founded the Church of Christ (Holiness) denomination. Under Mason's leadership,

 Women played an important role in the Azusa Street Revival and in the establishment of Pentecostal churches in the early twentieth century. William Seymour's wife, Jenny Evans Moore, was a co-pastor of the Azusa Street Faith Mission, which included female leaders from the start. The Azusa Street Revival, in fact, began due to the invitation of a woman named Lucy Farrow for Seymour to preach at a church Los Angeles. To learn more about influential women associated with early Pentecostalism, see Estrelda Alexander, *The Women of Azusa Street*.

the COGIC became—and remains today—the largest black Pentecostal denomination in America. One other early Pentecostal denomination was the International Church of the Foursquare Gospel, founded by "Sister" Aimee McPherson in 1927 in Los Angeles. McPherson, a white woman known for her dramatic evangelistic sermons and friendships with celebrities, founded the church on the four pillars of (1) salvation, (2) baptism in the Holy Spirit, (3) divine or miraculous healing, and (4) the imminent second coming of Christ. McPherson was a dynamic woman, and she regularly challenged gender and racial prejudices. She encouraged all races to attend her meetings, included African Americans on her staff, and admitted African Americans into the Christian school she founded.

In addition to the Church of God in Christ and the Church of the Foursquare, there were dozens of Pentecostal denominations and hundreds of Pentecostal churches that formed in the early twentieth century in America. While the Church of God in Christ became the single largest black Pentecostal denomination, the Assemblies of God (AG) became the largest white Pentecostal denomination. Though African Americans and Caucasians, along with many other ethnic groups, worshiped freely together at the Azusa Street Revival, they formed their own churches in the decades to come. There was also a division of Pentecostal churches into so-called trinitarian denominations and oneness denominations. The trinitarian denominations advocated that people should be baptized in the name of the Father, Son, and Spirit, whereas the oneness denominations believed it should be in the name of Jesus alone. These racial and theological divisions led to the fragmentation of Pentecostalism, which only proliferated in the years to come. More recently, America has witnessed the growth of many Pentecostal churches not directly tied to Pentecostal denominations. The so-called Charismatic Movement of the 1960s and 1970s emerged when countless Christians experienced spiritual gifts like speaking in tongues and miraculous healing but decided not to attend churches affiliated with historic Pentecostal denominations. Around the same time, white televangelists and radio personalities such as David du Plessis (1905–1987), Oral Roberts (1918–2009), Pat Robertson (1930–), and Paul Crouch (1934–2013) began bringing Pentecostal beliefs into the lives, churches, cars, and homes of millions across the world; yet few of those influenced by the movement became affiliated with the Pentecostal tradition. Meanwhile, there have been several very prominent black Charismatic and Pentecostal pastors in the past decades who have led some of the largest churches in America.

In the Word-of-Faith movement—which emphasizes material prosperity, charismatic Christianity, social action, and heavy use of technology and the media—pastors such as Frederick K. C. Price (1932–) and Creflo Dollar (1962–) have been at the cutting edge. Alongside Charismatic or so-called neo-Pentecostal preachers such as T. D. Jakes (1957–), these well-known television personalities demonstrate how far Pentecostalism has come in only a century of existence. Now the fastest segment of the church and steadied by leaders who are media sensations and magnets of wealth, Pentecostalism, in all of its ethnic and economic diversity, has come a long way from its humble abode on 312 Azusa Street.

Revivalism in America

In addition to the Pentecostal roots of the Azusa Street Revival, it is important to situate this revival in the centuries of revivals that have characterized America since the country's founding. Revivalism has been defined as an "emotional encounter with God through the Spirit."[7] There were several national revivals in America before the Azusa Street Revival. The first of these was the so-called First Great Awakening, which lasted from the 1730s to the 1750s. The major revivalist preachers were George Whitefield (1714–1770) and Jonathan Edwards (1703–1755). As with all major American revivals, fiery and impassioned sermons were met with emotional and ecstatic responses. The First Awakening underscored fundamental white American ideals such as religious liberty, personal choices, and anti-authoritarianism.

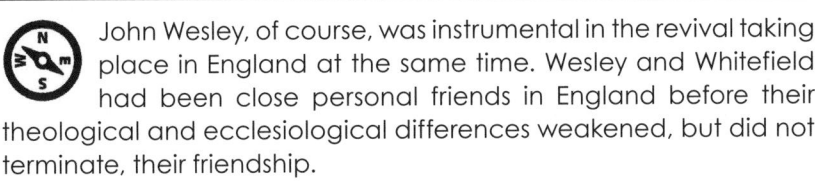

John Wesley, of course, was instrumental in the revival taking place in England at the same time. Wesley and Whitefield had been close personal friends in England before their theological and ecclesiological differences weakened, but did not terminate, their friendship.

Despite the cultural divide between African Americans and Caucasians, the democratic nature of revival appealed to and allowed the participation of slaves, who underwent "born again" experiences independently of their masters. As for Whitefield, his ambitious speaking schedule allowed him to preach before most of colonial America while his imposing oratory enshrined him as America's first celebrity. Jonathan Edwards, meanwhile, never left the East Coast but became famous for his evocative sermons and calm ruminations on the revivals taking place in America.

The Second Great Awakening lasted from the 1790s to the early 1800s. At one of its many venues, the Cane Ridge Revival in 1801 in Kentucky, thousands of Americans encountered God in an immediate and nontraditional way. Those who went to the revival were not disappointed. Charismatic preachers mesmerized audiences from their makeshift pulpits in the Kentucky woods. Marked by anti-creedalism, anti-authoritarianism, devotion, immediate conversion, individualism, and populism, the Second Great Awakening distilled the religious ethos of American culture and created space for religious innovation to develop. The tents at these "camp meetings" were filled with rich and poor, black and white. Many of the features of the white-led Second Awakening struck a chord with African spirituality. As Estrelda Alexander writes, the "jerking, rolling, fainting and shouting" of the revival paralleled "native . . . African traditional religion," the characteristics of which "became a hallmark of early Pentecostalism."[8] In terms of persons, Charles Finney (1792–1875), a white lawyer-turned-revivalist, exemplified the Second Awakening. Finney was pragmatic, populist, charismatic, anti-Calvinist, individualistic, and a master orator who pioneered evangelistic techniques that later revivalists such as Billy Graham (b. 1918) adopted. Finney was also an abolitionist and active in the Underground Railroad, which lent credibility to his message among African Americans. Another preacher during the Second Awakening was a freeman named Harry Hosier (1750–1806), commonly known as "Black Harry." Hosier occasionally accompanied Francis Asbury (1745–1816), one of the original bishops of the Methodist Episcopal Church (founded in 1784), on the speaking circuit. A highly regarded orator, Hosier preached to both black and white audiences.

Among mostly white audiences, the late nineteenth and early twentieth centuries produced some of the most prominent revivalistic preachers in American Protestantism. This includes D. L. Moody (1837–1899), Billy Sunday (1862–1935), and Billy Graham. Moody was a New Englander who converted to evangelical Christianity as a young shoe salesman in Boston. He spoke all over the world and founded the Moody Church in Chicago, Moody Publishers, and the Moody Bible Institute. Billy Sunday was a professional baseball player from the Midwest when he converted to Christianity and began itinerating. He had a colloquial style that appealed to the masses: "I don't know any more about theology than a jack-rabbit knows about ping-pong, but I'm on my way to glory."[9] Finally, Billy Graham is arguably the most famous Christian that America has ever produced. Graham rose to national attention in a revival he led in Los Angeles in 1949—only four decades after the Azusa Street Revival in the same city had simmered down. Perhaps due to the racial politics of the time, Graham's revival in Los Angeles was lauded by reporters while Seymour's was lampooned. The careers of these two revivalists provide remarkable contrast. Many white leaders attempted to discredit Seymour's teaching, and a few even attempted to take control of his congregation. In fact, after the flames of the Azusa Street Revival died down in the early 1910s, Seymour was largely forgotten among Pentecostal leaders. Billy Graham, meanwhile, has led revival campaigns in every part of the world and preached to more than 200 million seekers. Unlike Seymour, Graham is a public personality who has rubbed shoulders with celebrities and politicians alike, to the general acclaim of both the public and the media.

An Interracial Church

The last way the Azusa Street Revival illumines the history of Christianity in North America is by surfacing the complex story of race relations in American churches. Together with the frenzied activity on display every day in the early 1900s, visitors to the Azusa Street Mission took immediate notice of the free intermingling of different ethnic groups. There were no race or class distinctions. Although Asians and Hispanics living in America (as well as those from all parts of the world) were active participants at the mission, the mixing of African Americans and Caucasians during the "Jim Crow" days is what caught everyone's attention. It should not be overlooked that at this time in America, segregation laws kept black and white individuals separate from each other at drinking fountains, schools, public places, restaurants, and even in the military. Nor should it be overlooked that in "the ten years surrounding the Azusa Street Revival (1901–1911), 932 lynchings of African Americans took place in the United States."[10]

As for the media, the short April 1906 piece in the *Los Angeles Times* dwelled on race dynamics. The writer drew attention to the fact that "colored people" and "a sprinkling of whites" were present and that the mission's leader was a "colored brother."[11] Although the earliest chronicler of the Azusa Street Revival, Frank Bartleman (1871–1936) famously quipped that the " 'color line' was washed away in the blood"[12] at the Azusa Street

Mission, in truth the church meeting there in Los Angeles struggled to maintain a healthy multiracial dynamic during its short history. The bulk of the congregation was African American, but many prominent Caucasian leaders visited the mission. As mentioned above, a couple of these white leaders, such as Seymour's former mentor Charles Parham, attempted to wrest control of the church out of Seymour's hands. Jealous of the success of his former student and vocal about his opposition to black leadership, Parham strongly criticized both Seymour and the Azusa Street Revival. (His attempts to strong-arm Seymour were only thwarted after he was arrested and charged with immoral conduct.) Due to the criticism of trusted colleagues such as Parham as well as the severe denunciations of prominent white church leaders across America, we can see some of the scars that racism left on William Seymour. In 1915, several years after the heyday of the Apostolic Faith Mission and after Seymour had turned his attention to creating new missions across the country, he wrote in his manual called *Doctrines and Disciplines* that only a "colored man" would be permitted to serve as a bishop or vice bishop.[13] This policy was meant to guarantee that blacks would not be overtaken by white leadership in the new missions.

Division between white and black Christians has been a continual theme of American church history, and Estrelda Alexander bluntly remarks that "race has been an issue in American religion since the first shipment of African slaves arrived on the shores of North America [in 1619]."[14] Indeed, as African American orator Frederick Douglass (1818–1895) said in a speech given in 1861, it would seem that "color makes all the difference in the application of our American Christianity."[15] Unlike the type of slavery practiced in many other cultures, slavery in America was racially based and has generated countless social and systemic problems. Although many slaves attended and were "saved" at revivals in the eighteenth and nineteenth centuries, American denominations restricted preaching licenses and ordination to white men. Plantation-based missions among African Americans began in the 1800s, though slaveholders were reluctant to expose their slaves to abolitionist agendas for fear that the liberating message of Christianity preached among slaves would undermine the institution of slavery. Yet beyond the watchful eye of the white man, slave religion was nurtured by the Negro spirituals, rhythmic dancing, dreams of liberation, and biblical stories passed on orally from generation to generation.

The Baptist and Methodist churches were the traditions that soared to new heights among African Americans, since these two traditions were more accessible and less rigid than the Episcopal and Presbyterian churches. They were also more supportive of abolitionism. By the late 1700s, African Americans made up about a fourth of the Methodist Church. This mixing of blacks and whites in churches created great friction, and we can see this tension in one of the first of many church splits in the Methodist tradition. After converting to Christianity under Methodist preaching in 1777, the African American slave Richard Allen (1760–1831) eventually purchased his freedom and received preaching opportunities in the newly created Methodist Episcopal Church. In 1786, the Philadelphia-based Saint George's Church invited Allen to preach at a 5:00 A.M. service for African Americans. Because this service brought a flux of black Christians into the white congregation, racial hostilities ran high. The next year, while in prayer along with other black Christians such as Absalom Jones (1746–1818) at the church, Allen was physically removed due to his presence in a part of the church only designated for white people. Thereafter, Allen became pastor of Bethel Church of Philadelphia in 1794, one of the first African American churches. Although originally a Methodist Episcopal Church, the church became one of five churches to create the African Methodist Episcopal Church in 1816 in order to protect its property from lawsuits (from Saint George's) and secure theological freedom. The church has since become known as "Mother" Bethel African Methodist Episcopal Church, and Allen served as the bishop of the denomination.

Many African American churches in the nineteenth century, such as the African Methodist Episcopal Church, were actively involved in abolitionism and in the Underground Railroad. Sojourner Truth (1797–1883) and Harriet Tubman (1822–1913) were two of the most influential African American women involved in social activism at this time. Their colleagues Frederick Douglass and William Lloyd Garrison (1805–1879) were powerful apologists of abolitionism who called for the end of slavery and rallied together people of like mind. Throughout the nineteenth century, palpable racial tensions were flaring not only in churches but in society as a whole. The Civil War raged between 1861 and 1865, testing the resolve of the struggling nation. The rhetoric of the Civil War constantly invoked the name of God. Both sides remained absolutely convinced—even after the war—that God favored their side. Indeed, depending on the side of the Mason-Dixon Line on which the preacher lived, the Bible clearly affirmed or resolutely condemned slavery. Needless to say, the issue of racism and slavery caused countless church splits, the results of which are evident to this day. No major church denomination escaped unbroken.

Although "the Civil War solved the religion and slavery problem . . . it did not solve the religion and race problem."[16] Lamentably, the church was just too divided to offer a united voice. Then something happened in the middle of the twentieth century. In 1954, the landmark *Brown v. Board of Education* ruling by the Supreme Court mandated the integration of white and black children in public schools. A year later, Rosa Parks (1913–2005) famously refused to vacate her seat for white passengers in the colored section of a public bus until the police arrested her. The African American community then launched a successful boycott of public buses in Montgomery, Alabama, from 1955 to 1966, sparking the civil rights movement.

It was at this time that a twenty-six-year-old African American pastor at a small Baptist church in Montgomery rose to prominence as the spokesperson for the boycott. Four days after Rosa Parks was arrested, Martin Luther King Jr. (1929–1968) preached to a packed Southern audience:

> We are not wrong in what we are doing. If we are wrong, then the Supreme Court of this nation is wrong. If we are wrong, the Constitution of the United States is wrong. If we are wrong, God Almighty is wrong. If we are wrong, Jesus of Nazareth was merely a utopian dreamer and never came down on earth. If we are wrong, justice is a lie. And we are determined here in Montgomery to work and fight until justice runs down like water, and righteousness like a mighty stream.[17]

In less than ten years, King would receive the Nobel Peace Prize and gain international admiration for his humanitarian efforts. However, his assassination in 1968 demonstrated that, despite the end of slavery for almost a century, racism in America was still rampant.

As an heir to the civil rights movement, Black Theology has attempted to give shape to a Christian theology that seriously considers the plight of the marginalized. It draws inspiration from Christianity, the Black Power movement, the civil rights movement, and Marxism. Though labeled "Black Theology," its most outstanding spokesman, James Cone (1938–), argues that Black Theology "has little to do with skin color. Being black means that your heart, your soul, and your body are where the dispossessed are."[18] Black Theology is an example of contextual theology, which maintains that all theology is yoked to a specific cultural and historical context, meaning that Western theology—often envisioning itself as normative of all Christian expressions—is simply one theology among many other valid ones. But Black Theology has not been without its critics. James Cone's brother, Cecil Wayne Cone, wrote a critique of his brother's work in a book titled *The Identity Crisis in Black Theology*, which argued that James Cone was too dependent on European and European American thinking rather than African and African American sources. There have been other criticisms of the movement from within, indicating the great diversity of the African American Church.

Although the issue of race has been discussed at all levels of society, American churches are still highly divided across racial lines. This is even true of most Pentecostal churches, despite the fact that the Azusa Street Faith Mission, the fountain of Pentecostal Christianity, was established as an interracial ministry. In fact, at the conclusion of their more recent study of Protestant evangelicalism in America, authors Michael Emerson and Christian Smith noted in their book *Divided by Faith* that evangelicalism "does more to perpetuate the racialized society [of America] than reduce it" and that there are no "specific solutions [in place] for ending racialization."[19] In America at least, the church's loss of oneness has impaired its ability to offer any united resistance against racial injustices. In contrast to the Nicene Creed's declaration in 381, the church in America appears to be "many" rather than "one." And it will likely be some time, if ever, before churches across America will say in unison with a Pentecostal pastor from Tennessee, "Glory to God! Makes me feel good to see whites and colored praisin' God together."[20]

Conclusion: From Warehouse to World

Near the corner of Azusa and San Pedro Streets in downtown Los Angeles stands a modest plaque commemorating the Azusa Street Revival. The plaque celebrates the Apostolic Faith Mission's seminal role in the birth and dissemination of the worldwide Pentecostal movement. Although we are a mere century removed from its past, the building where Pentecostalism was born is strangely a distant memory to many of those who live and work in the neighborhood. The formerly abandoned warehouse sheltered Spirit-led believers for twenty-five years before it was demolished in the summer of 1931 as a termite-ridden eyesore. In reality, the street was but a glorified alleyway and never more than one block.

Since the Azusa Street Revival, Pentecostalism has spread to every part of the inhabited world. Not only is the former warehouse no longer at the center of the movement, notes Pentecostal theologian Amos Yong, but Pentecostalism in North America "is no longer at the vanguard of what

God is doing through this movement in the world."[21] Scholars dispute the exact numbers, but a little more than a century after the Azusa Street Revival occurred, Pentecostals number more than 600 million. With the Holy Spirit as its shepherd and the world as its parish, it seems that the sky is the limit for Pentecostal Christianity.[22]

 ## Questions for Personal Exploration

1. Why do you think Pentecostalism is the fastest-growing Christian tradition in the world? What are some of the challenges it will face?
2. Go back and read through each of the longer quotes from primary literature in this chapter. What is the sense you get as you read through them?
3. Why do you think Christianity has experienced more revivals in the United States than perhaps in any other country during the history of the church?
4. How should the church in the United States deal with issues of race in a concrete way? Why do you think churches in North America are still very segregated along ethnic and racial lines? How does this relate to the issue of the catholicity of the church?

 ## Resources for Deeper Exploration

Anderson, Allan. *To the Ends of the Earth: Pentecostalism and the Transformation of World Christianity.* Oxford: Oxford University Press, 2014.

Butler, Jon, Randall Balmer, and Grand Wacker. *Religion in American Life: A Short History.* 2nd ed. Oxford: Oxford University Press, 2011.

Hollenweger, Walter. *Pentecostalism: Origins and Developments Worldwide.* Peabody, MA: Hendrickson, 1997.

Noll, Mark. *God and Race in American Politics: A Short History.* Princeton, NJ: Princeton University Press, 2008.

Pinn, Anne, and Anthony Pinn. *Fortress Introduction to Black Church History.* Minneapolis: Fortress Press, 2002.

Robeck, Cecil, Jr. *The Azusa Street Mission and Revival.* Nashville: Thomas Nelson, 2006.

Yong, Amos. *The Spirit Poured Out on All Flesh: Pentecostalism and the Possibility of Global Theology.* Grand Rapids: Baker, 2005.

👓 Notes

1. Harvey Cox, *Fire from Heaven: The Rise of Pentecostal Spirituality and the Reshaping of Religion in the Twenty-First Century* (Reading, MA: Addison-Wesley, 1995), 51.

2. "Weird Babel of Tongues," *Los Angeles Times*, April 18, 1906.

3. Estrelda Alexander, *Black Fire: One Hundred Years of African American Pentecostalism* (Downers Grove, IL: InterVarsity), 20.

4. Alexander, *Black Fire*, 16.

5. Dale Irvin, "Black Pentecostalism, Black Theology, and the Global Context," in *Afro-Pentecostal Pentecostalism: Black Pentecostal and Charismatic Christianity in History and Culture*, ed. Amos Yong and Estrelda Alexander (New York and London: New York University Press, 2011), 233–34.

6. "On Working Out Our Own Salvation," *The Works of John Wesley* (Peabody, MA: Hendrickson, 1986), 6:508.

7. Allan Anderson, *To the Ends of the Earth: Pentecostalism and the Transformation of World Christianity* (Oxford: Oxford University Press, 2013), 11.

8. Alexander, *Black Fire*, 66.

9. George Marsden, *Fundamentalism and American Culture*, 2nd ed. (Oxford: Oxford University Press, 2006), 130.

10. Alexander, *Black Fire*, 249.

11. *Los Angeles Times*, "Weird Babel of Tongues."

12. Frank Bartleman, *Azusa Street: An Eyewitness Account* (Alachua, FL: Bridge-Logos, 1980), 59.

13. This is in articles F and G, respectively, of the manual. Quoted in Douglas Jacobsen, *Thinking in the Spirit: Theologies of the Early Pentecostal Movement* (Bloomington: Indiana University Press, 2003), 65.

14. Alexander, *Black Fire*, 19.

15. Quoted in Mark Noll, *The Civil War as a Theological Crisis* (Chapel Hill: University of North Carolina Press, 2006), 68.

16. Mark Noll, *God and Race in American Politics: A Short History* (Princeton, NJ: Princeton University Press, 2008), 176.

17. Quoted in Albert Raboteau, *Canaan Land: A Religious History of African Americans* (Oxford: Oxford University Press, 2001), 110.

18. James Cone, *Black Theology and Black Power* (Maryknoll, NY: Orbis, 1997; original ed. 1969), 151.

19. Michael Emerson and Christian Smith, *Divided by Faith: Evangelical Religion and the Problem of Race in America* (Oxford: Oxford University Press, 2000), 170–71.

20. Quoted in Vinson Synan, *The Holiness-Pentecostal Tradition: Charismatic Movements in the Twentieth Century* (Grand Rapids, MI: Eerdmans, 1997), 183.

21. Amos Yong, *The Spirit Poured Out on All Flesh: Pentecostalism and the Possibility of Global Theology* (Grand Rapids: Baker, 2005), 32.

22. Anderson, *To the Ends of the Earth*, 1–3.

Thomas Baker exhibition at the Fiji Museum in Suva. Photo used by permission from the Kerr Family.

Chapter 11

A Boot in Fiji Illumines the History of Christianity in Oceania

At 3:00 P.M. on July 20, 1867, an English-born Australian missionary entered a tiny village in the western highlands of Viti Levu in Fiji. He was accompanied by a Fijian minister, local teachers, and several Christian students. They were unarmed. The missionary immediately sent a message to the chief of the Navosa tribe, requesting to meet with him. Without much delay, the chief arrived with a retinue of armed tribesmen. The chief promptly sat down on a stone in the village courtyard. The missionary approached the chief alongside his native guide, shook his hand, ceremoniously presented the tooth of a whale, asked him to embrace Christianity, and requested freedom of passage to the next village.

In defiance of local custom, the chief did not present any food to the visitors that night, so they went to bed hungry in the chief's hut. The next morning, which was the Sabbath, the missionary led his companions in their daily devotion of prayer, singing, and Scripture reading before leaving the village in haste before he had time to drink his morning coffee. The local chief guided the missionary and his companions out of the village. They had just set out on the trek when the local villagers attacked them. Within minutes, all but one or two of the Christians were dead. The missionary, the Reverend Thomas Baker (1832–1867), received a sharp blow to the head and died instantly. The dead bodies were then piled high in the village, chopped to pieces, roasted, and eaten. According to one of the cannibals, "We ate everything but [Baker's] boots."[1]

The Story of a Boot

The Reverend Thomas Baker was born in Sussex, England, but moved with his family to the English colony of New South Wales (now Australia) as a child. After learning the trade of shoemaking, he had a dramatic conversion experience in 1849 and began preparing for the ministry. He left for Fiji in 1859 with a new wife. There, he lived with his wife for seven years as a Methodist missionary. At this time in Fiji, Protestants were making great strides in the evangelization of the islands and in the translation of the Bible into local dialects. Baker had difficulty learning the local language and sometimes clashed with his superiors at the mission, but he firmly believed that God had called him to be a missionary.

Ironically, Baker's fateful missionary journey in the highlands of Fiji in 1867 happened just after he had requested and received approval to return with his wife and children to Australia for a furlough. Unknown to him, the trip was to be his last act as a missionary. After entering some friendlier villages, Baker and his associates proceeded to a village known for its hostility. In fact, they did this against the clear advice of Chief Waqaliqali, who had predicted "dire consequences if Baker proceeded"[2] to this hostile tribe. Although the local Christians with Baker feared the chief's words, the foreign missionary disregarded the advice of the chief and proceeded to the next village.[3] That evening, just two days before being killed and eaten, he wrote a letter to his wife, who was expecting his quick return so they could return to Australia:

> I find we are about midway across the land and have resolved to go all the way now [that] I am so far in. I had thought of this before I left you but did not name it, because I knew you could not endure the thought of my going away for so long a time. But I have only decided this evening to go. And I do so because, first, I want to do the people good. Second, because I believe there is no great obstacle in my way. And third, because if I do not go now, I shall never go. . . . People are becoming Christian all around and there is only here and there a town that is not *lotu* [Christian]. We start early in the morning. . . . I anticipate no difficulty except in this place. If they do not *lotu* [accept Christianity] I believe they will not venture to kill me.[4]

Less than forty-eight hours later, the people of Navosa were feasting on his body. News of Thomas Baker's death reached Sydney, Australia's *Empire* newspaper at the end of September. The article reported that Baker and the local Christians with him had been killed by a tribe of men who accompanied the missionaries on their way to preach the gospel to a new village. It said, "After [the tribe] had killed them all they dragged the bodies into town, and piled them up one on another, placing the Rev. Mr. Baker's body on the top of the pile, while they made the ovens hot in which to roast them."[5]

Although the report of the deaths of Thomas Baker and his Fijian associates is seemingly straightforward, their deaths have never been fully resolved. There are roughly three theories on why they were killed and cannibalized. The first is that Baker did not follow ancient tribal ritual procedures when meeting with the chief of the Navosa people. It has been alleged that Baker and his associates met the Navosa people and performed the *tabua* (whale's tooth) ceremony in an unfit location. This seems unlikely, however, given that Baker was accompanied by many local Fijians who were well accustomed to following cultural protocols in their homeland. Besides, Baker had taken part in many of these ceremonies. The second theory is that Baker touched the head of the chief when he attempted to remove either his comb or his hat from the chief's head. The touching of a chief's head was a great cultural blunder. It merited death. Today this theory is firmly supported by the village that killed Baker in 1867, so it is quite possibly accurate. The last theory is that Baker and his companions, whether they violated any cultural protocols or not, unknowingly signed their death warrants the moment they entered the village. It has been argued that a chief of another tribe who had previously converted to (and later rejected) Christianity told the chief of the Navosa people to kill any missionaries who sought to convert his people out of fear that the Christian religion would spread. To ratify the ritual killing, the Christian tribal chief supposedly sent the chief of the Navosa a whale's tooth.

Whatever the exact cause of Baker's death, there are several artifacts that give testimony today to the life of this missionary. The Fiji Museum, in the capital city of Suva, has a permanent exhibition dedicated to Thomas Baker and the few remaining artifacts connected to his death. There is a whale tooth (*tabua*) that possibly was sent to the tribe that killed Baker from a Christian tribe of Fiji as a bargaining chip to persuade the chief to kill any missionaries who entered his village. There are also some utensils, including a fork, used to eat Baker and his associates, as well as the Bible he used to give devotions on the morning of his death.

The most intriguing items on display at the museum, however, are the pair of disconnected leather soles of Baker's boots. Legend has it that the villagers who ate Baker unsuccessfully attempted to boil down his shoes but never could soften the leather. Ironically, Baker had been apprenticed to a shoemaker in New South Wales as an adolescent. However, his conversion in 1849 prompted him to leave the trade of shoemaking and enter the vocation of foreign missions. At any rate, the display at the Fiji Museum contains a modest description of the boots belonging to the missionary: "The remains of Mr. Baker's boots recovered from near where he was murdered after the event."[6] Many teeth marks give evidence of the cannibals' attempt to eat the soles, but now they are safely enclosed behind glass.

Christianity in the Isles

The soles of Thomas Baker's boots and the story of his fateful encounter with the Navosa people throw light on the history of Christianity in Oceania by introducing the Christian faith in the Pacific islands, highlighting the relationship between foreign and domestic missionaries, and surfacing the cultural clashes between Western missionaries and native inhabitants. Beginning with the first, no other part of the world is as connected to the seas as Oceania. This region, in fact, is as defined by water as it is by land. As for the term *Oceania*, it is a recent one that has come to include what has also been called Australasia or the South Pacific. Oceania can be divided into four major groupings: Australia, Melanesia, Micronesia, and Polynesia (see table 11.1). Combined, these four major regions make up thousands of islands.

The earliest contact between Westerners and Pacific islanders occurred in the spring of 1521, when Spanish explorer Ferdinand Magellan (1480–1521) landed in Micronesia. Cultural clashes ensued between locals and Westerners, and Magellan and his men barely made it out alive before being killed soon afterward in the Philippines. Although there were other excursions by Westerners into Oceania after that time, it was Captain James Cook (1728–1779) of the Royal British Navy who put the Pacific islands on the map. The journals and exploits of Captain Cook inspired pious

Table 11.1 Division of Oceania into Major Regions

General Name of Area	Largest Countries	General Population	Primary Religious Affiliation
Australia	Australia and New Zealand	27,670,000	Protestant (nominal)
Melanesia	Fiji, Papua New Guinea, and Solomon Islands	7,580,000	Protestant
Micronesia	Guam (USA), Kiribati, Federation of Micronesia	562,000	Roman Catholic
Polynesia	French Polynesia, Samoa, and Tonga	665,000	Protestant

Christians in England to form the London Missionary Society (LMS) to evangelize the many people groups Cook and his crew discovered.

We may fittingly classify the settlement and Christianization of Oceania into different waves of colonization and evangelization. Europeans established colonies and transported their own into the newly discovered lands;

> The English missionary William Carey was probably the most famous leader of Protestant missions in the English-speaking world in the late eighteenth and early nineteenth centuries. Born a generation after Captain Cook, Carey was at the forefront of the Protestant endeavor to evangelize all of the world in obedience to the Great Commission.

some who made the journey were missionaries intent on converting the local inhabitants. Historian Ian Shevill notes the similar waves of Western missionaries onto the different islands of Oceania: "First came the shock-troops of the Non-Episcopal Churches [such as the Methodists], then the occupation army of the creedal churches, either Anglican or Roman, and finally the camp followers, the independent Missions, Seventh Day Adventists, and the American Sects. Each brought its contribution to evangelization, each wave being led by heroes with different methods."[7]

Although some missionaries had been active as early as the seventeenth century, it was not until the nineteenth century that missionaries like Thomas Baker entered Oceania in full force. The different Protestant agencies were followed by Catholic missionaries. Due to rivalry and an overabundance of islands, denominations evangelized different people groups to the effect that many nations today are Catholic or Lutheran or Seventh-Day Adventist, for instance, as a result of the work of missionaries from France, Germany, and the United States, respectively.

By the turn of the twentieth century, most of Oceania had been Christianized. Bibles had been translated into local languages, inhabitants could read and write, new schools were established, and advances in health care and medicine had generated healthier and longer lives. By the end of World Wars I and II, indigenous churches were widespread on the islands. In fact, it is arguable that Oceania is the most Christianized region on earth. Though it houses a very small percentage of worldwide Christianity, Oceania is full of churches, and the culture is overwhelmingly Christian in orientation. In many ways, to be from the Pacific islands today means to be at least nominally Christian.

Foreign and Domestic Missionaries

A second way that the boots of Thomas Baker illumine the history of Christianity in Oceania is by drawing attention to the important relationship between foreign and native missionaries. Although the incident of 1867 causes many of us to focus on the death of Thomas Baker, seven additional men from Oceania were killed and eaten. All of these men were native Fijians who died for their Christian faith, just as Baker did. The death of one missionary and seven native Christians reminds us that the evangelization of Oceania would not have taken place without both foreign and domestic missionaries. In Fiji, for instance, the first missionaries to the islands were not Westerners but men from French Polynesia. Their names were Faaruea, Fuatai, and Taharaa. These missionaries entered Fiji in 1830 and planted the first church. "Native" missionaries, though coming from

Although several missionaries highlighted in this chapter were cannibalized for their Christian faith, there were many other missionaries—both domestic and foreign—who were well received and graciously welcomed among villagers.

distant Pacific islands and speaking different languages, still had a much better understanding of local customs than Western missionaries did. For example, whereas Westerners tended to think individualistically, Pacific islanders thought collectively. Evangelization, they intuitively understood, had to be communally based in order to be effective and long-lasting. There was no merit in evangelizing individuals irrespective of the community, and Christianization of tribes was effective inasmuch as it took this dynamic into consideration.

We see evidence of the collective conversion of one region of Oceania after a famous battle that took place in Fiji. The Battle of Kaba was fought on April 7, 1855, in the small island of Bau, just off the east coast of the major Fijian island of Viti Levu—the opposite side from where Thomas Baker would be killed a dozen years later. In the battle, the two major forces were led by Ratu (an honorific title akin to "Chief") Cakobau (1815–1883) and Ratu Mara. Because Cakobau had just converted to Christianity the year before, the war became an epic struggle between Christianity and paganism. The nearby leader of Tonga, King George (1845–1893), who was a new Christian ally, reinforced Cakobau's victory over his pagan rival as well as the cessation of a twelve-year war against the chiefdom of Rewa. A few days before the battle, a religious service had been conducted featuring the famous battle language of Ephesians: "Put on the whole armor of God, so that you may be able to stand against the wiles of the devil" (6:11).[8] Upon Cakobau's victory, a "chief summed up the reaction of many Fijians: 'The *lotu* [that is, the Christian religion] is true or Kaba would not have been taken.'"[9]

After Cakobau defeated his pagan enemies, the new Christian values he had been taught led him to reject a time-honored practice that followed battle. In an unusual act of generosity, Cakobau pardoned his captives rather than eating them. Cakobau's defeat of Rewa paved the way for the adoption of Fiji by Great Britain in 1874, and Cakobau signed the deed and was heralded as the King of Fiji. In this decisive battle, Christianity prevailed in Fiji, and paganism receded. Evidence of the importance of this battle and of Cakobau's victory is that the Methodist Church in Fiji multi-plied from 5,000 members in 1852 to 125,000 in 1874.[10] The tribal culture of Fiji interpreted this victory as proof that the Christian God was supreme and that the people owed allegiance to this God for their triumph. Thou-sands converted to Christianity within months of the battle.

The Battle of Kaba was important in Fiji's history in many ways, but it would not have taken place without the construction and use of countless canoes by the warriors of Fiji and Tonga. The making and navigation of canoes was, in fact, recognized by both foreign and domestic missionar-ies as essential to Christian evangelism. When the first Westerners entered Oceania back in 1521, for instance, they noted the agile canoes in which the local people moved stealthily from island to island. These boats soon became the unsung heroes of the evangelization of Oceania.[11] Missionary ships such as the *Southern Cross* in Melanesia, the *Morning Star* in Micro-nesia, and the *John Williams* in Polynesia transported both domestic and foreign missionaries across the mighty waves of the Pacific Ocean in order to spread the faith. The English missionary John Williams (1796–1839) became famous for his ship-making skills and sea adventures. Although a seasoned missionary who had years of experience traveling in his boats from island to island, he was killed and eaten by cannibals in Vanuatu about three decades before Thomas Baker experienced the same fate in Fiji.

A Clash of Civilizations

The last way that the boots of the Rev. Thomas Baker illumine the history of Christianity in Oceania is by giving concrete proof of the cultural rivalry between Western Christians and local inhabitants. Speaking about the death and eating of Thomas Baker, Fijian prime minister Laisenia Qarase went so far as to say that what really occurred that fateful day "was a clash of civilizations."[12] Cultural clashes between natives of Europe and Oceania are traceable to the very first encounters between the two people groups, and we can see a clear example of this with the colonization of Micronesia in the seventeenth century.

Spanish Catholics began colonization of Micronesia in 1668. The Spaniards originally used Guam as a stopping point for their galleons as they made the long sail from Mexico to Manila, Philippines—their base in Asia. But a priest named Father Diego Luis de San Vitores (1627–1672) felt burdened to share the gospel with the locals of the islands there, which he named the Mariana Islands. San Vitores took several priests and soldiers to Guam and arrived in June. He learned the language of the Chamorro people, those native to the islands, aboard ship so he could immediately

> The Spanish were most successful in establishing foreign colonies and missions in the Americas, but they also colonized and evangelized parts of Africa and Asia in addition to Oceania. Regardless of the region, the Christian tradition that Spain introduced was Catholicism.

preach and sing songs. After he preached his first sermon in Chamorro, "more than fifteen hundred people came forward to accept Christ."[13]

Despite the success, cultural clashes between the Spanish and the Chamorro people began in earnest. To begin with, the Chamorro nobility did not want priests to teach and baptize the common people. They believed Catholic Christianity was reserved for them alone. San Vitores, however, rejected such a mind-set and went about baptizing both common people and nobility. His first noble convert was Chief Kepuha (d. 1669). This aged chief gave the priest some land on which to establish the first Catholic church—against the wishes of many other noblemen. Chief Kepuha died shortly thereafter and was buried at the church. San Vitores's resolve to bury the chief at a church rather than under a latte stone (a pillar looking like a giant mushroom) was a major cultural faux pas.

The next major cultural clash occurred when San Vitores and his fellow priests began baptizing infants. Eventually a rumor was started that the Spanish priests baptized children in poison. As for the Catholic sacrament of baptism, although adult baptism was typically delayed until instruction was complete, Catholic priests always baptized babies in the belief that water baptism removed original sin and put them under the grace of God. Unfortunately, the baptism of many children who were already deathly sick—and who consequently died—reinforced the rumor. Parents began hiding their babies and clawing away the priests like angry mother bears. To make matters worse, a drought hit Guam in 1670. Naturally, the people blamed this devastating phenomenon on the Spaniards. Finally, a priest presided over a wedding ceremony between a Spanish soldier and a baptized Chamorro girl in violation of local marriage customs. The girl's father killed the priest, and the Spaniards then killed the father.

The cultural clashes between the Spanish and the Chamorro people led to an all-out war. In 1671, Chief Hurao (d. 1672) gave a famous speech to his people to strengthen their resolve to defeat the Catholic Spanish intruders and remove them from the islands:

> The Spanish would have done better to remain in their country. We have no need of their help to live happily. Satisfied with what our islands furnish us, we desire nothing. The knowledge which they have given has only increased our needs and stimulated our desires. They find it evil that we do not dress. If that were necessary, nature would have produced us with clothes. They treat us as gross barbarians. But do we have to believe them? Under the excuse of instructing us, they are corrupting us. They take away from us the primitive simplicity in which we live.[14]

Chief Hurao was arrested, but unrest between the Chamorro and Spaniards continued. On September 11, 1671, around two thousand Chamorro warriors attacked the walls surrounding where the Spaniards lived. San Vitores released Chief Hurao as an act of mercy despite protests from the Spaniards. The battle then abated and a truce was reached, but resentment festered. In April 1672, San Vitores baptized the infant of a chief and was immediately murdered by the chief along with Chief Hurao. The two chiefs speared San Vitores's body with lances and smashed in his head. Historian Robert Rogers summarizes the death and burial of San Vitores by the chiefs:

> They removed the clothing and crucifixes of the dead men and spread burning coals to consume the pools of blood from the bodies. Mata'pang [a chief and the father of the baptized infant] smashed a small cross that San Vitores wore, but he kept a large ivory crucifix of the priest's. Next they dragged the naked bodies down to the shore, placed them in a proa, and tied stones to their feet. After paddling over the Tumon reef in the proa, they tossed the bodies overboard. According to some accounts, San Vitores surfaced twice to grasp the proa's outrigger but was pried off each time by Mata'pang.

When San Vitores rose a third time and grasped the boat's stern, Mata'pang smashed the priest's head with a paddle. Father Diego Luis de San Vitores then sank for the last time into the crystalline water of Tumon not far from where [Ferdinand] Magellan had first dropped anchor in the Pacific a century and a half earlier.[15]

Not surprisingly, it was only a month before a Spanish soldier killed Chief Hurao out of vengeance. Meanwhile, the Spanish-Chamorro War lasted until 1695. The next wave of Catholic evangelization of Guam was as fierce as it was successful. Today, in fact, a shrine stands on the spot where San Vitores was killed, and the majority of the population of the Mariana Islands is Catholic. "In many places," writes one historian of Micronesia, the church "is the dominant institution in the daily life of the people."[16]

Conclusion: The Holy Clash Continues

The conflict evident in the Spanish evangelization and colonization of Guam in the late 1600s was a foreshadowing of the clashes between Western Christian civilization and Pacific religious culture for centuries to come. To be sure, there were many commonalities between the different groups, and real and authentic friendships were made, but misunderstandings and suspicion abounded. Speaking about the cultural clash between the Rev. Thomas Baker and the Navosa tribe that killed and cannibalized him two hundred years after the skirmishes between the Spaniards and Chamorro people, the prime minister of Fiji said, "Those who killed and ate the Reverend Thomas Baker and his believers would have felt they were defending themselves against threats to their established ways."[17]

The occasion for the prime minister's comments was a forgiveness ceremony initiated by the people whose ancestors murdered Baker and his companions. In November 2003, bare-chested Fijian warriors in the remote village of Nabutautau adorned in grass skirts with painted faces asked forgiveness from the living descendants of Thomas Baker for killing and eating him. At the six-hour ceremony, villagers presented whales' teeth, woven mats, and a sacrificed cow to the descendants to atone for the sins the villagers had committed in 1867. A dozen villagers reenacted the death of Baker with the very ax that had split Baker's skull. Baker's descendants took part in a symbolic act of cutting the so-called chain of curse that had shackled the village in poverty and obscurity for the past 136 years. Thomas Baker's great-great-grandson accepted the village's apology in front of the great-great-grandson of the chief who had ordered Baker's death. Journalists from all parts also attended. The *Sunday Post* reported:

> A prayer was said asking for the blessing of the land and its people from that day onwards. The sunny day was . . . broken minutes later as dark clouds hovered around the village, opening up for intermittent rain. The people of Navatusila took it as a sign . . . that their apology had been accepted and acknowledged by the Almighty. They linked the events to a passage in the Bible, in the Old Testament, in 2 Chronicles, Chapter 7:14: If my people . . . humble themselves and . . . turn from their wicked ways, then I will hear them from Heaven, will forgive their sins, and will heal their land.[18]

The death of Baker and the ceremony 136 years later introduce all kinds of questions about the nature of the church as it is incarnated in particular cultures. In short, all four marks of the church are tested every time it enters a new culture. How will the church maintain oneness despite various denominations and personalities attempting to steer the isolated churches in different directions? How will the church remain holy when those at the helm are broken human beings full of biases and other shortcomings? How will the church learn from and remain accountable to Christians from other parts of the world and other traditions when they are overburdened with their own regional issues? And how will the church remain true to the teachings of the apostles while also responding in appropriate and reasonable ways to present realities that Jesus and his disciples never faced? Each community of faith will answer these questions in its own ways, but they will not go away anytime soon.

Questions for Personal Exploration

1. Why do you think Oceania has become one of the most Christianized regions on the planet? What accounts for this adoption of Christian culture, given the divergent forms of Christian churches that have entered the islands in the past couple of hundred years?

2. Go back and read through each of the longer quotes from primary literature in this chapter. What is the sense you get as you read through them?

3. How do you think you would attempt to bring together the many varieties of Christian traditions in Oceania if you were appointed to such a position? Where would you begin, and what types of encounters do you think you would face?

4. How large a role do you think culture plays in Christianity? What is the relationship between Christianity and culture supposed to be?

5. How would you respond if you were invited by a foreign village to atone for its sin of murdering one of your ancestors? Would you accept the apology? How do you think this apology would affect the welfare and religious views of the village?

 Resources for Deeper Exploration

Breward, Ian. *A History of the Churches in Australasia*. Oxford: Oxford University Press, 2004.

Farhadian Charles, and Robert Hefner, eds. *Introducing World Christianity*. Oxford: Wiley-Blackwell, 2012.

Fischer, Steven Roger. *A History of the Pacific Islands*. 2nd ed. New York: Palgrave Macmillan, 2002.

Matsuda, Matt. *Pacific Worlds: A History of Seas, Peoples, and Cultures*. Cambridge: Cambridge University Press, 2012.

Rogers, Robert. *Destiny's Landfall: A History of Guam*. Honolulu: University of Hawaii Press, 1995.

Thornley, Andrew. *Exodus of the I Taukei: The Wesleyan Church in Fiji, 1848–1874*. Suva, Fiji: Institute of Pacific Studies, University of the South Pacific, 2002.

Tippett, Alan. *The Deep Sea Canoe: The Story of Third World Missionaries in the South Pacific*. South Pasadena, CA: William Carey Library, 1977.

👀 Notes

1. "Eaten Missionary's Family Get Apology," *BBC News*, November 13, 2003, http://news.bbc.co.uk/2/hi/asia-pacific/3263163.stm.

2. Quoted in Andrew Thornley, *Exodus of the I Taukei: The Wesleyan Church in Fiji, 1848–1874* (Suva, Fiji: Institute of Pacific Studies, University of the South Pacific, 2002), 345.

3. Ibid., 345.

4. Quoted in ibid., 346.

5. "Murder of the Rev. Thomas Baker, Wesleyan Missionary, and Seven Native Teachers at Fiji," in *Sydney Empire*, September 27, 1867, accessed at Papers Past, http://paperspast.natlib.govt.nz/cgi-bin/paperspast?a=d&d=HBWT18671021.2.13.

6. Description at the exhibit in the Fiji Museum in Suva, Fiji.

7. Ian Shevill, *"Pacific Conquest": The History of 150 Years of Missionary Progress in the South Pacific* (Sydney, Australia: Pacific Christian Literature Society, 1949), 7.

8. Thornley, *Exodus of the I Taukei*, 79.

9. Ibid., 80.

10. Matt Tomlinson, "The Generation of the Now: Denominational Politics in Fijian Christianity," in *Christian Politics in Oceania*, ed. Matt Tomlinson and Debra McDougall (New York: Bergahn, 2013), 79.

11. For more about the spread of the gospel by these canoes, see Alan Tippett, *The Deep Sea Canoe: The Story of Third World Missionaries in the South Pacific* (South Pasadena, CA: William Carey Library, 1977).

12. Nick Squires, "Fijians Killed and Ate a Missionary in 1867; Yesterday Their Descendants Apologised," *(London) Telegraph*, November 14, 2003, http://www.telegraph.co.uk/news/worldnews/australiaandthepacific/fiji/1446723/Fijians-killed-and-ate-a-missionary-in-1867.-Yesterday-their-descendants-apologised.html.

13. Lawrence Cunningham and Janice Beaty, *A History of Guam* (Honolulu: Bess, 2001), 83.

14. Quoted in Geoffrey Gunn, ed., *First Globalization: The Eurasian Exchange, 1500-1800* (Oxford: Rowman & Littlefield, 2003), 194–95. Historian Robert Rogers suggests that the speech was made up by a French Jesuit based on similar speeches. See Robert Rogers, *Destiny's Landfall: A History of Guam* (Honolulu: University of Hawaii Press, 1995), 52.

15. Rogers, *Destiny's Landfall*, 55.

16. Francis Hezel, "Christianity in Micronesia," in *Introducing World Christianity*, ed. Charles Farhadian (Oxford: Blackwell, 2012), 241.

17. Squires, "Fijians Killed and Ate a Missionary in 1867."

18. *Sunday Post*, November 14, 2003. Quoted in Jacqueline Ryle, *My God, My Land: Interwoven Paths of Christianity and Traditions in Fiji* (Surrey: Ashgate, 2010), 67.

PART

3

How We Study Church History—Method

The study of church history is one of the most exciting adventures on which one can embark in academia. Unlike some disciplines, the field of church history is constantly in flux and never static. New discoveries of ancient articles drive us toward novel interpretations and revisions of old ones. The geographic extent of church history is immense, encompassing the entire globe. Its ongoing engagement with new cultures, people groups, and worldviews propels it into new spheres of influence and new orbits of thought.

Although we sometimes regard history as synonymous with the past, they are two very different things. As church historian Justo González writes, "History is not the same as the past. The past is never directly accessible to us. The past comes to us through the mediation of interpretation. And that interpreted past is history."[1] Church history is the subjective interpretation of objective articles connected to Christianity. As mentioned in the first chapter, articles of the past include relics, pictures, buildings, apologies, autobiographies, Bibles, journals, letters, poetry and fiction, tomes, decrees, weapons, vessels, clothing, frescoes, statues, sculptures, murals, graffiti, icons, cemeteries, castles, palaces, court records, wills—and many other things as well.

In this part, which consists of only one chapter, we will allow a medieval scholar to guide us along the path of theological method—how we study church history. Specifically, we will focus on how to research and write a paper on church history. As in many disciplines, critical thinking, good research skills, and a sound ability to synthesize the information we uncover will be the ingredients necessary to thrive in the academic field of church history. With that said, let us turn now to fifteenth-century Italy on the eve of one of the greatest exposés in all of church history!

1. Justo L. González, *The Changing Shape of Church History* (St. Louis: Chalice, 2002), 2.

Thirteenth-century fresco depiction of Constantine "donating" his empire to Sylvester and the church. From Santi Quattro Coronati in Rome, an ancient basilica dedicated to four Christian saints who died as martyrs.

Chapter 12

A Medieval Forgery Illumines How to Write a Paper on Church History

t was the spring of 1440. Not unlike professors today, an academic from Italy was wandering from place to place in search of a stable position. By most accounts, the man was not very pleasant. He was, however, a master philologist and textual critic. His area of specialization was the Latin language—a tongue long since dead other than in the mouths of Catholic priests or in classical pagan and Catholic writings. This man made many enemies, for he had a habit of "not only [going] against the dead, but against the living as well."[1] For the time being, the man turned his critical mind to a document believed to have been more than a thousand years old. He made a shocking discovery. Not only was the document he investigated not written when it claimed to have been written, but it was completely fraudulent. The man, Lorenzo Valla (1407–1457), had just exposed the "the most infamous forgery in the world,"[2] let alone in church history. The techniques he used to expose the document prompted one scholar to conclude that with him, "the Middle Ages [had come] to an end."[3]

The Story of a Medieval Forgery

The so-called *Donation of Constantine* was a masterful and deeply influential forgery that had tricked unsuspecting Christians for centuries. With little exception, this document had been universally regarded as genuine until Lorenzo Valla disproved its authenticity. Valla's exposure of the forgery formed a tidal wave in the theological world. It is no accident, for example, that German reformer Martin Luther (1483–1546) "began to distance himself fully from Rome"[4] immediately after reading Valla's book in February 1520 and accepting his argument in full. The discredited *Donation of Constantine* provided the tangible proof of the Catholic Church's corruption for which Luther had been searching. Luther's outrage at the forgery was manifest in a letter he wrote to George Spalatin (1484–1545) on February 24, 1520:

> I have at hand Lorenzo Valla's proof . . . that the Donation of Constantine is a forgery. Good heavens! What darkness and wickedness is at Rome! You wonder at the judgement of God that such inauthentic, crass, impudent lies not only lived but prevailed for so many centuries, that they were incorporated in the Canon Law, and (that no degree of horror might be wanting) that they became as articles of faith. I am in such a passion that I scarcely doubt that the Pope is the Antichrist expected by the world, so closely do their acts, lives, sayings, and laws agree. But more of this when I see you. If you have not yet seen the book, I shall take care that you read it.[5]

Whatever the exact relationship between the Protestant Reformations and Valla's exposé of the forgery, it is certain that King Alfonso V of Aragon (r. 1416–1458), under whom Valla served as a secretary in Naples from 1435 to 1448, used the document that Valla wrote to his own advantage in his territorial disputes with the pope. Valla's discovery, it seemed, was opening up a new chapter in the story of the Christian West.

The *Donation of Constantine* claimed to be written at the end of the life of Emperor Constantine (r. 306–337). At this time, the document alleges, the aging emperor was cured of leprosy by the then-reigning pope, Sylvester (r. 314–335). Constantine wrote the document in appreciation of the "supreme Pontiff and Pope universal" and out of a desire to extend Constantine's favorable powers upon all succeeding generations of popes:

> If a document falsely applies a famous name to a document, it is said to be pseudepigraphic. It should be remembered that Constantine is commonly regarded as the first Christian emperor of the Roman Empire, whose patronage of Christianity dramatically altered the shape of Western civilization. Given this, critical historians would be very curious as to why his name would be used in connection to the Donation of Constantine.

And to our Father, the Blessed Sylvester, supreme Pontiff and Pope universal, of the city of Rome, and to all the Pontiffs, his successors, who shall sit in the seat of the Blessed Peter even unto the end of the world, we by this present do give our imperial Lateran palace, then the diadem, that is, the crown of our head, and at the same time the tiara and also . . . the purple mantle and scarlet tunic, and all the imperial [clothing]. . . . We decree, moreover, as to the most reverend men, the clergy of different orders who serve that same holy Roman church, that they have that same eminence, distinction, power and excellence, by the glory of which it seems proper for our most illustrious senate to be adorned; that is, that they be made patricians and consuls, and also we have proclaimed that they be decorated with the other imperial dignities.[6]

The *Donation of Constantine* stated in no uncertain terms that the emperor gave all temporal authority to the Catholic Church. Such authority enshrined the power of the Catholic Church, and the pope in particular,

 There is no exact date for the Middle Ages. It is historically the time period in the West dividing the Classical Period from the Modern Period, an epoch dating very generally from the fifth to the fifteenth centuries CE.

as utterly unassailable. During the Middle Ages, the papacy acquired the so-called Papal States, which were large parts of land in Italy, and commanded forces much like a commander or emperor did. Medieval historian R. W. Southern writes that medieval popes "dreamed of a militia of St Peter, of secular rulers obedient to command, of knights sworn to faithful service, of mercenaries paid to act as agents of the church. Popes claimed the sole right of initiating and directing wars against the unbelievers . . . raised armies, conducted campaigns, and made treaties of peace in defence of their territorial interests. They put the whole weight of their spiritual and temporal authority behind these efforts."[7]

To those who disobeyed the emperor's clear directions in the *Donation of Constantine*, condemnation and everlasting punishment followed. As the forgery aggressively concluded, those who ignored or rejected this decree "shall be subject and bound over to eternal damnation, and shall feel the holy ones of God, the chief of the apostles, Peter and Paul, opposed to him in the present and in the future life, and he shall be burned in the lower hell and shall perish with the devil."[8] Reflecting and adding to the punishments found at the end of the book of Revelation (22:18), this document understandably commanded credence for centuries.

Scholars today believe that the *Donation of Constantine* was written in eighth-century Rome at the height of disputes between the papacy and earthly rulers. Such a context makes perfect sense for the writing of a document claiming that all temporal power remained in the hands of the pope and that anyone who questioned him would face the wrath of the almighty apostles Peter and Paul. This document remained unquestioned until the development of a new culture in the West that relied more on critical thinking and intense textual scrutiny than on tradition. The medieval Italian thinkers Dante (1265–1321) and Nicholas of Cusa (1401–1464) had previously questioned the authenticity of the *Donation of Constantine*, but it was Lorenzo Valla who offered irrefutable proof that the document was a forgery.

As for Lorenzo Valla, he held a clerical status in the Catholic Church and received a benefice (earnings) but never entered the priesthood. He sired three children out of wedlock with his sister's servant. In 1440, while in the coastal town Gaeta, Italy, Valla wrote his exposé of the *Donation of Constantine* as a scathing critique against the Catholic Church and its current pope, Eugenius IV (r. 1431–1447). Valla, in his own words, deplored the "various contradictions, impossibilities, stupidities, barbarisms, and absurdities" of the *Donation of Constantine* as well as the "blockheads" who used the document to support papal authority.[9]

Getting Started on a Research Paper

Lorenzo Valla's exposure of the greatest forgery in church history was what historian Alfred Hiatt called "a turning point in the history of criticism."[10] By using the most advanced literary techniques available coupled with critical thinking, solid research, and not a little bravado, Valla successfully uncovered what had eluded so many other readers before him. To be sure, Valla is not to be commended for all of his actions, for he was a bitter man with many enemies and pounced on his foes with gusto. Yet the spirit of his training as a Renaissance humanist can be useful in illumining how we may research and write papers on the history of Christianity. In the following section, we will discuss some of the most essential features of researching and writing about church history. We will allow Valla's exposure of the *Donation of Constantine* to guide us in the collection of sources, the formulation of an argument or thesis, and the overcoming of barriers when writing.

Collecting Sources

In the study of history, different types of sources aid our understanding of the past. They are commonly called "primary" and "secondary" sources. Both are necessary in the researching and writing of church history papers. It's been my experience that students tend to err on the side of citing secondary sources, but this is perhaps misguided.

Primary sources, which are artifacts or documents dating from the time period you are studying, are like anchors of the past. Such sources can be anything from frescoes from the Catacombs of Callixtus in Rome (second to fourth centuries) to John Bunyan's (1628–1688) allegorical novel *The Pilgrim's Progress*. All scholarship is built on locating, deciphering, and interpreting primary sources. Naturally, scholars disagree on their findings, but they all agree that primary sources are essential to the study of church history. How do you obtain primary sources? For most of us, we obtain them through libraries and other online sources. We leave the actual discovery of primary sources to archaeologists. And once archaeologists locate and uncover these primary sources, the findings are sent to art and architectural historians, epigraphists (those who study inscriptions), and professional translators, who decode and translate the documents. Publishers then publish what is found in articles, reports, and books for us to read and interpret.

Secondary sources comment on primary sources. They are often written by scholars. In our discipline, church historians are professional scholars who debate their interpretations of primary sources. Among secondary sources, there are two general kinds: popular or devotional and academic or scholarly. In general, the more academic a source, the more specialized it tends to be. Monographs are scholarly books that target a theme or topic in depth. A good secondary source does not necessarily have to be written by a person with a PhD, but certain publishers are more academically rigorous than others. Academic presses associated with universities, for instance, mostly publish works written by learned professors and based on the best primary and secondary scholarship available. So-called popular or devotional writings can be just as helpful as scholarly works, but they have a different aim. They are not always peer-reviewed and often are written from the perspective of a certain theological confessional stance.

Whatever types of sources you may use in researching a paper, we should have Lorenzo Valla in mind when it comes to thinking critically. All publications are written from a certain perspective, and it is up to us to determine what this perspective is and whether it illumines the topic at hand or obfuscates it.

In addition to primary and secondary sources, historical works express many perspectives, or schools of thought. Any given secondary work of scholarship, for instance, may focus on the history of ideas, history of missions, biographical history, political history, art and architectural history, ecological history, feminist history, military history, history of science, social history, history of religions, and history of doctrine or dogma. Each of these schools of thought allows researchers like you and me to better understand a particular historical context. For instance, a good research paper on Lutheranism will discuss not only its theological views but also how the movement arose, what ethnic groups are predominant, what its views are on money or marriage, and what type of art it produces. Although everyone tends to lean in the direction of either so-called intellectual or social history—that is, history emphasizing ideas or that emphasizing social realities—both are important. Good research papers understand that history is always told from a certain perspective, and that it is necessary to read scholarship from multiple perspectives and schools of thought in order to accurately reconstruct what really happened in the past.

Formulating an Argument

It was not until I was a graduate student that I realized that all academic papers are supposed to be written in defense of some type of argument or have what many academic fields call a "thesis." Before that time, I naively assumed that simply researching and narrating the life of a person, event, or time period was sufficient. What professors really want to see in a church history paper, however, is not simply a report of something that happened but your unique interpretation that sheds new light on the past. Rather than knowing *what* happened, for example, we want to know *why* it happened the way it did and not another way. For your argument or thesis, you may imagine that you are a courtroom lawyer who has to convince the judge (that is, the professor) for or against something. For instance, it is one thing to narrate the life of Thomas Aquinas, but it is something different to advance a new theory about his life that helps us better understand him and his context. The ability to formulate an argument from something you may not know very much about requires familiarity with your topic and the ability to filter through a lot of extraneous information. After selecting a topic of research (based on interest, availability of sources, and the guidelines established by the professor), your next step is to read and interpret your sources (both primary and secondary) before allowing them to help you formulate an argument.

Your argument or thesis should then be clearly stated in the first paragraph or introduction of your paper. Your argument can vary greatly depending on your topic. For instance, your argument could be "In this paper, I will demonstrate that Byzantine art is based on pagan Greco-Roman art in the following three ways." Such an argument should only be formulated after you have chosen a research topic related to Byzantine art and after you have read the information relevant to this topic. Here is another possible example of a thesis: "This paper argues that Augustine's interpretation of the book of Romans influenced the development of the Reformed tradition in two ways." Notice that the thesis is not the same as the research topic, which, in this case, would be Augustine's interpretation of the book of Romans vis-à-vis the Reformed tradition.

After stating your thesis in the introduction, you should then organize your ideas into sensible and accessible categories. For instance, in a paper dedicated to showing how Julian of Norwich's view of motherhood shaped her theology, you could organize the paper into the following parts in addition to an introduction and conclusion: (1) the life and times of Julian of Norwich, (2) the relation of her thinking to that of other female mystics, and (3) an examination of her revelations. Your thesis should shape how each of these categories is designed, and it should guide the reader. For each section of the paper, be sure to include only information that pertains to your argument and remove parts that that may be interesting but otherwise irrelevant to the thesis you are seeking to prove.

Overcoming Barriers

Now that you have done the research and have formulated an argument for your paper, it is time to write your first draft. At this point, you may find it helpful to construct an outline with the major points you would like to

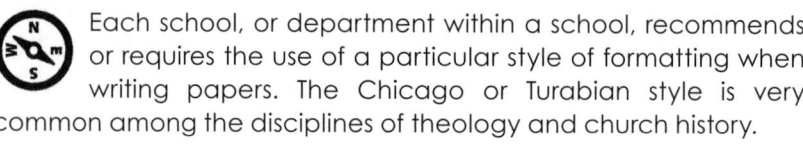

Each school, or department within a school, recommends or requires the use of a particular style of formatting when writing papers. The Chicago or Turabian style is very common among the disciplines of theology and church history.

make. As you write the paper, you will need to overcome any number of barriers to good writing, such as avoiding generalizations, neutralizing your biases, diversifying the types of sources you use, narrowing your research even further, focusing on the essential points of the topic, and not drowning the paper in needless details. In the midst of overcoming all of these barriers, I am assuming, of course, that you have followed standard rules of grammar and adopted an accepted form of citation designated by your school, such as MLA or Turabian.

When seeking to overcome barriers in writing, it is important to avoid generalizations and neutralize biases. Naturally, we all make mistakes and are all biased to some extent, but scholarship is based on critical reflection and sound argumentation. Scholarship follows facts, whether we like them or not, and we must be fair with the results we uncover. By way of example, we could imagine how a well-meaning Protestant believer, whether intentionally or not, generalizes poorly about Catholic doctrine. For instance, I have read papers that say something like this: "All Catholics believe that the pope cannot make mistakes." This sloppy statement is wrong on two fronts. First, Catholic doctrine does not teach that the pope must always be right or that he cannot make mistakes. Rather, it teaches that when the pope speaks *ex cathedra*—that is, in an official capacity (which, by the way, has not been attempted for decades)—he cannot err doctrinally or morally. Second, Catholics demonstrate a wide variety of beliefs on every imaginable topic, including the extent, if at all, of the pope's authority. A more accurate way to phrase the statement would be "Official Catholic doctrine teaches that the pope cannot err on matters of faith or morals when he speaks in an official capacity as head of the Roman Catholic Church." In a similar way, it is equally inaccurate to write something like "Catholics worship Mary." Not only is this a generalization, but it also smacks of bias. Although it is certainly possible that some Catholics have and do "worship" Mary, such a practice is rejected by official Catholic teaching. The sentence, if it is to be salvaged at all, should be amended to something like this: "The following group worships Mary despite official Catholic teaching to the contrary," followed by a credible source giving testimony to this statement.

Another set of steps to follow in the process of overcoming barriers is to further limit your research, use only the best available sources, and omit unnecessary details from your writing. These are not easy steps. Because I have discussed sources already, I will merely underscore here that our papers are only as good as our sources, so we must locate and use primary and secondary sources astutely and discriminately. Besides locating and interpreting the best sources (which is an art that only develops over time as you sharpen your research skills), one of the most challenging parts of researching and writing is limiting your paper to pertinent information. After you have read several articles, books, and online sources, there is a temptation to dazzle the reader with all the data you have uncovered. Writing an excellent paper, however, is not just about demonstrating how much you know but also about filtering and synthesizing what you know. As a general principle, a more focused research paper is better than one that is too broad. For instance, if you would like to explore the history of Methodism in the United States, think about focusing your research on an individual, event, or specific time period of American Methodism, rather than tackling the whole history. A good paper is like a sculpture. What begins as a large and unwieldy piece of wood is slowly but continually refined and sculpted into a distinct piece of art that has a clear and identifiable shape. For your paper, keep this adage in mind: If any given sentence or thought does not contribute to your overall thesis, remove it. Clarity of thought and conciseness trumps unmanageable amounts of data and extraneous quotes. Keep the paper simple, clear, and focused.

Conclusion: Becoming a Budding Church Historian

Today, no popes cite the *Donation of Constantine* as evidence of their authority. And an entire church tradition, Protestantism, contains millions of believers who no longer affiliate with the Catholic Church. What's more, the king under whom Lorenzo Valla served used the latter's work to bolster his claims of Italian territory against arguments to the contrary coming from the current pope. What do these historical facts have in common? Whether or not we support all of Lorenzo Valla's accusations and techniques, his critical eye demonstrates how influential and powerful scholarship can truly be.

For most of us, it is unlikely that we will ever discover a forgery on the magnitude of that discerned by Valla, but we build upon the sound techniques of analysis, critical thinking, historical criticism, and language studies to help us understand one of the most fascinating subjects in all of academia. Our brief survey of how to research and write a paper on church history derives, in part, from the humanistic approach of Lorenzo Valla, demonstrating once again how much we rely on those Christians who have walked before us and how much we have to learn from those of the past. I hope you have gained a new appreciation of church history as we have explored this topic in depth. May your future endeavors in the history of Christianity yield great fruit in years to come!

 ## Questions for Personal Exploration

1. If you were giving a presentation on how to write a solid church history paper to beginner students, what things would you emphasize? What would be some pitfalls to avoid?
2. What part do you think Lorenzo Valla's exposure of the *Donation of Constantine* as a forgery played in the development of Protestantism?
3. How do the different specializations of historians shape what they focus on when writing, and how can you recognize their strengths and weaknesses?
4. What are some checkpoints to consider when finalizing a church history paper?

 ## Resources for Deeper Exploration

Bradley, James, and Richard Muller. *Church History: An Introduction to Research, Reference Works, and Methods.* Grand Rapids: Eerdmans, 1995.

Cooper, Derek. *So You're Thinking about Going to Seminary: An Insider's Guide.* Grand Rapids: Brazos, 2008.

Pazmino, Robert. *Doing Theological Research: An Introductory Guide for Survival in Theological Education.* Eugene, OR: Wipf & Stock, 2009.

Valla, Lorenzo. *On the Donation of Constantine.* Trans. G. W. Bowersock. Cambridge, MA: Harvard University Press, 2007.

Yaghijian, Lucretia. *Writing Theology Well: A Rhetoric for Theological and Biblical Writers.* London: Continuum, 2006.

☯ Notes

1. This is from the opening part of his attack against the document in Lorenzo Valla, *On the Donation of Constantine*, trans. G. W. Bowersock (Cambridge, MA: Harvard University Press, 2007), 3.

2. Johannes Fried, *Donation of Constantine and* Constitutum Constantini*: The Misinterpretation of a Fiction and Its Original Meaning* (Berlin: de Gruyter, 2007), 1.

3. Quoted in Alfred Hiatt, *The Making of Medieval Forgeries: False Documents in Fifteenth-Century England* (Toronto: University of Toronto Press, 2004), 167.

4. Fried, *Donation of Constantine*, 31. See also David Whitford, "The Papal Antichrist: Martin Luther and the Underappreciated Influence of Lorenzo Valla," *Renaissance Quarterly* 61 (2008): 29–30.

5. Quoted in Preserved Smith, *The Life and Letters of Martin Luther* (Boston: Houghton Mifflin, 1914), 73.

6. "The Donation of Constantine," in *The Treatise of Lorenzo Valla on the Donation of Constantine*, trans. Christopher Coleman (New Haven, CT: Yale University Press, 1912), 13, 15.

7. R. W. Southern, *Western Society and the Church in the Middle Ages* (London: Penguin, 1970), 19.

8. "The Donation of Constantine," 19

9. Valla, *On the Donation of Constantine*, 9, 57.

10. Hiatt, *The Making of Medieval Forgeries*, 167.